DREAM INTERPRETATION BY EXAMPLE

REAL DREAMS WITH DETAILED EXPERT ANALYSIS

VOLUME ONE

By

WAYDE GILCHRIST

Part of the *Real Dreams* Series

Copyright ©2009 by Wayde Gilchrist. All Rights Reserved.

Published by The Idea Store Inc.

ISBN-13: 978-0-9843385-1-1

No part of this book may be used or reproduced in any manner whatsoever without written permission except in the case of brief quotations embodied in critical articles and reviews.

Warning and Disclaimer : While every effort has been made to be accurate, the author and publisher assume no responsibility or liability for errors made in this book. This book is not completely comprehensive. Some readers may wish to consult additional books for advice.

The author and publisher make no representations about the suitability of the information contained in the book for any purpose. The material is provided "as is" without warranty of any kind.

The information in this book is offered with the understanding that is does not contain medical, legal, financial, or other professional advice. Individuals requiring such services should consult a competent professional.

Contents

INTRODUCTION   9
    BUILDING THE BRIDGE 9
    BENEFITS OF UNDERSTANDING DREAMS 10
    WHY ANOTHER DREAM BOOK 10
    ABOUT THE DREAMS IN THE BOOK 10

CHAPTER 1 – DREAMS 101   13
    WHERE DREAMS COME FROM 13
    OUR BIGGEST FEARS BECOME NIGHTMARES 15
        Cheating Husband 16
        Cheat and Cheat Again 16
    WISH FULFILLMENT 17
        The Flying Dream 17
        The Girl of My Dreams 18
    WE ALL DREAM 18
    REMEMBERING DREAMS 19
    WHAT IT TAKES TO BE A DREAM INTERPRETER 19

CHAPTER 2 – ELEMENTS   21
    WATER DREAMS 21
        Rising Water 21
        Streets of Water 22
        Streets of Dirty Water 24
    EARTH 25
        Earthquake Warning 25
        Wheelbarrow 25
        Serial Killer 26
    AIR 27
        Cloud Animals 27
        Tornado 27
    FIRE 28
        Dock on Fire 28
        House on Fire 28

Distant Fires 29

CHAPTER 3 – DREAMS IN MOTION 31

CARS AND DRIVING 31
   Rocks in a Stream... 31
   Speeding Cars 33
   Car Leaking Fluid... 34
TRAINS 34
   NYC Subway... 35
   Train Dream... 35
PLANES 36
   Airplane Bumper Cars 36
   Emergency Landing 36
BOATS 37
   The Paddle Boat... 37
   Boat on Murky Water 38

CHAPTER 4 – DREAMING IN COLOR 39

RED 40
   Red Fluid... 40
   Red Lottery Tickets.. 40
   Treasure Find... 41
ORANGE 42
   Orange Road... 42
   Out of Body 43
YELLOW 44
   Dark Angel... 44
   Wrapped In Yellow 44
GREEN / PINK 45
   Wifely Duties 45
   Stuck in Throat... 46
   Green Water 46
   Irish Club Band.. 47
BLUE 48
   Blue Snake.. 48
PURPLE 48
   Angry Spirit.. 49
WHITE 49

 Baby with a Scratch 49
 Playing Alone 50
BLACK AND WHITE 51
 Black and White 51

CHAPTER 5 – WHO ARE THESE PEOPLE AND WHY ARE THEY IN MY DREAM?   55

PREGNANCY 56
 Pregnant 56
 Out of the Womb 57
BABIES 57
 A Baby 57
CHILDREN 58
 Twenty-seven Children 58
 Roadblock 61
BOSS / CO-WORKERS 61
 The Boss and a Ring 62
 Remote Control 62
CELEBRITIES 65
 Reality Star 65
 Ambitions Shot Down 66
HAIRDRESSERS 67
 Hairdresser 67
PEOPLE WHO HAVE PASSED AWAY 67
 Dead or Alive? 68
 Commemorative Plaque 68
POLICE / SOLDIERS 69
 Sister Getting Married 69
 I Hate Nazis 71
 Keeping the Past in the Basement 72

CHAPTER 6 – ANIMAL DREAMS   77

DOGS ARE #1 77
 Thanksgiving is Going to the Dogs 78
 Pit Bulls 78
 Viscous Dog 79
CATS 80

Cat Attack	*80*
BIG CATS – LIONS AND TIGERS	81
Lions Outside	*81*
Lion at School	*81*
Cougar	*83*
White Tiger	*84*
BIRDS	85
The Owl and the Cloud	*86*
MICE	86
Mice	*86*
BUGS AND SPIDERS	86
Bugs and Spiders	*87*
FISH	87
Calm water	*87*
Dishonesty	*88*
HORSES	89
Wild Horse	*89*
BEARS	90
Growling Bears and Dogs	*90*
Boyfriend's Produce	*91*
SNAKES	92
Snake Dreams	*93*
ALLIGATORS / CROCODILES	94
Alligators	*95*
ELEPHANTS	95
Elephant	*95*
SEA LIONS	96
Tornadoes and an Aquarium	*96*

CHAPTER 7 – BUILDINGS AND PLACES   99

HOUSES / MANSIONS	99
Demons in the Basement	*99*
Haunted House	*100*
APARTMENT	102
Moving	*102*
SKYSCRAPERS	102
Terrorist Plane	*102*
TREES / FOREST	104

  Growing Up *104*
  Christmas Tree *105*
 Mall 106
  Driving Toward Mall *106*
  Plane Crash at Mall *107*
 Bank 108
  Bank Robbery *108*
 Las Vegas 110
  What Happens in Vegas *110*
 Hospital 110
  In the Hospital *111*
  Nick Nolte *111*
 New York City 113
  Chased by Terrorists *113*
 Stadium 114
  Murder, Murder *114*
 Bathroom 115
  Daughter's Pictures *115*
 School 117
  Weddings *117*
 Harbor 118
  Safe Harbor *118*
 Warehouse / Garage 120
  Warehouse *120*

CHAPTER 8 – EVERYTHING ELSE   123

 Health Dreams 123
  History Repeating Itself *123*
  Explosion from the Sea *125*
  Teeth Falling Out *126*
 Food Dreams 126
  Fast Food *126*
  Cheesecake *128*
  Friend's Hamburger Dream *128*
 Word Phrases 128
  Taylor Wilson *129*

INDEX OF DREAM SYMBOLS   131

Introduction

Welcome to the world of dreams.

Dreams are like a different world. The regular laws of physics from the waking world don't necessarily apply. People who are dead are suddenly alive again. The dream world is a strange place. But you are no stranger to it. Everyone enters the world of dreams several times per night. We're all regular visitors.

With so much experience, it would be logical to think that we should all be experts on the subject of dreams. But we're not. Not at least consciously.

Subconsciously, that's a different matter. Our subconscious mind is the architect of our dreams. It is the ultimate dream expert. However, our conscious mind tends to ignore our dreams.

Our conscious mind is comfortable with the waking world. It likes when the laws of physics apply and things are logical. So, it shuts off when we start dreaming. This keeps our waking and dream worlds separate. This is a good thing. Otherwise, we may forget which world we are in and jump off a roof, believing we can fly. So it is for our own good that understanding our dreams requires a bit of conscious effort.

Building the Bridge

To understand dreams, we need to bridge the waking and dream worlds. The first step for building this bridge is to remember our dreams. The first chapter of this book gives some tips and advice for remembering dreams.

The second step is to learn the dream language. That is where the rest of this book comes in. The easiest way to learn a new language is by example. No one taught you how to speak your first language, you learned by hearing others. By reading this book you will learn to understand the language of dreams by seeing how real dreams are interpreted.

Benefits of Understanding Dreams

Once you build the bridge into your dreams you will discover the answers to many mysteries about yourself.

- Why you make certain choices
- Where you lack confidence
- What really worries you
- What you really want
- How you became the person you are
- Why you are not the person you want to be

Why Another Dream Book

At last check, there were 3,602 *different* dream dictionaries for sale on Amazon.com.

This book is not another dream dictionary. If you look up a word in a dictionary, you get the meaning of the word. But, you don't get the meaning of the whole story. You have to see how the words relate together in a sentence to understand a complete thought. And you have to put all the sentences together to understand the entire message.

In this book you will study complete dreams and see how to infer their meanings from the relationships between the individual symbols.

About the Dreams in the Book

The dreams in this book were all posted on the Internet by people asking for interpretations. Each one of these dreams were personally interpreted by me and posted on my web site: **www.askthedreamexpert.com.** I never met nor do I know any of the dreamers. In most cases, unless it is mentioned by them, I don't even know basic information such as their location, occupation or age.

The dreams are presented as they were posted. Some of the dreams are very short—a sentence or two. Others are quite long and involved. To keep them anonymous, I removed names or indentifying information. If the dreamer replied with some feedback about the interpretation, I included that information. The titles for each dream were created by me.

Every day, new and fascinating dreams are being posted and interpreted on our web site. This book is the first volume in what is intended to become a series. Post your dreams on our website, and maybe you'll see them in my next book.

WAYDE GILCHRIST
wayde@askthedreamexpert.com

Chapter 1 – Dreams 101

Where Dreams Come From

Dreams come from a portion of our mind called the subconscious. It is called the sub-conscious because it exists deeper inside than the conscious mind. Most people think of themselves as their conscious mind. When awake, we mostly use our conscious mind to guide us through the day. We use it to plan our schedule, solve problems, and communicate. We normally refer to the activities of our conscious mind as our thoughts. Through our thoughts we choose what we want.

But our thoughts don't operate alone. When deciding what to have for dinner we use our thoughts to review our options, like chicken, steak, fish, but we use our feelings to make the choice. In our thoughts we ask our subconscious mind to make the decision. We ask, "What do I *feel* like eating for dinner, the chicken, or the fish?" And that is how we decide. Most of the time, the way we make decisions is by asking our subconscious. We may believe that our conscious mind is in control, but in reality we give that power to our subconscious.

Our feelings are what really determine how we live our life, and they don't come from the conscious mind. Even though they come from the subconscious, we experience our feelings when we are awake because the subconscious is active all the time. However, the conscious mind, stops being active when we go to sleep and are no longer thinking.

It is during sleep when we go exploring in our subconscious mind. What we find there is what creates our dreams.

Although we can experience, and sometimes recognize, our feelings when we are awake, we usually don't know why we feel the way we do. For example, why do we feel attraction to one person, but not to another? The answer is that our feelings are a consequence of our experiences.

Within our minds is a vast storage unit, bigger than the biggest computer hard drive ever created. It records everything we experience. More than just memories, this storage unit also records our feelings. As you live your life in the present, your subconscious compares your current experience with all its past memories. It finds ones that are similar and creates an emotional response based upon the feelings and outcomes associated with the past experiences. The reason you are attracted to someone is that something about them reminds you of someone in your past who you loved. That is why we often end up marrying someone like our father or mother.

Our recorded past experiences have taught us the likely outcomes of certain situations. Consciously recalling all of these experiences and their consequences each minute of the day would overload our thoughts and leave us unable to function. Instead, the subconscious creates a feeling that enables us to respond instantly to any situation without deliberating on the details of the past.

We can also be taught to have certain responses without having the experience. Our parents and teachers try to impart the wisdom of their experience without us having to live it ourselves. For example, you have probably never been hit by a car, but you look both ways when crossing the street because you are afraid of being hit. This is an example of something your parents taught you as a child and remains a strong influence upon your behavior.

We go through life behaving and reacting according to what has been recorded in our mind, without consciously knowing all the details. We just trust our feelings.

When we dream our subconscious is playing back this mental programming. It creates life-like situations built around our beliefs and concerns.

Our Biggest Fears Become Nightmares

More than anything else, we dream about our fears. We all have them. Some come from past experiences, some from our parents, and some from books, television or movies. It doesn't matter where they came from because the subconscious treats them all the same. If you accept that there are people or things that could possibly harm you, then you will feel frightened when you are faced with them.

Fear can paralyze us. It stops us from taking risks and from putting ourselves into new and unfamiliar situations. It always seems safest just to keep with the same old routine and not venture outside of the box. However, we can't grow and evolve spiritually unless we take on new challenges, or at least allow them to occur. It is for this reason that we must face and manage our fears. Fortunately, dreams help us to do just that. Our dreams present us with imagery so vivid and real that we forget that we are sleeping safe in our bed. So in our dreams we feel emotions in a very real and powerful way; just as if the dream was really happening.

In our dreams our subconscious creates the scene, the characters, the dialog, and the action for a complete mini-movie with you in it. If it's a horror movie then your subconscious is creating a safe way for you to experience your fears. You may be wondering why it would do this. Dreaming about a plane crash certainly isn't going to help you get over your fear of flying. The answer is that your dreams are nothing more than a mirror. What you see when you sleep is simply a reflection of your current emotional state. Your emotions are the real basis for your decisions and the way your life turns out. Our dream periods are the only time we get a clear picture of our true feelings.

As a child our nightmares are about monsters or being chased because we feel insecure and vulnerable. As an adult our nightmares are about losing the things we love most. Parents commonly dream about bad things happening to their children. Other nightmares are about adult issues such as relationships or job loss.

A very common nightmare is regarding infidelity.

CHEATING HUSBAND

> I have had a dream that my husband had an affair and it was with my friend actually.

If you dream about your spouse having an affair it DOES NOT mean that they are. Your subconscious is just expressing your fear that you are afraid that they might. It could turn out that there is an affair, but your subconscious is not telling you this.

However, the subconscious retains a memory of every time you were hurt. So, if you try to forgive someone for an affair, keep in mind that you may not be able to stop the nightmares. You won't be able to get your subconscious to forget the past.

CHEAT AND CHEAT AGAIN

> In the last three months I started having dreams that my spouse is cheating on me, and I could see the face and body of the other woman but never actually connect it to anyone I know. I know if I am having this dream it means that I'm just worried about it. However, a month after those dreams started, he did cheat on me and the face in my dreams was his ex, who he cheated on with me.
>
> After that the dreams just stopped. We went our separate ways and about one month later we got back together. Now I am having dreams about me, him, and another girl taking a shower together and we were considered his "two spouses". I got really upset so I told him he had to pick one or the other. At first he hesitated, but he picked me. One other dream I had was

me, him and a friend running away from somebody and our friend got shot and that made us closer in my dream.

The dreams showed that the dreamer could not convince her subconscious to trust him. He has proven himself to be a cheater, and the dreamer's subconscious has recorded the pain. So, her subconscious will continue to warn her about him because it has learned from past experience that she will probably be hurt again. The friend getting shot is a symbol for getting hurt. So, a part of her thinks that since he hurt her once he now feels bad and wouldn't do it again.

Wish Fulfillment

Fortunately, not all our dreams are nightmares. On the contrary, some are so fantastic and enjoyable that we don't want them to end. Consider this common dream:

THE FLYING DREAM
I dream often that I have to get off the ground and I can fly. I have a hard time to take off because I'm afraid but I gain courage and I lift straight up and start flying, I always feel like I'm escaping from something or someone I don't know what or who because I'm always by myself.

In this classic dream, the dreamer wants more than anything to escape his current environment. But he feels powerless to do so. His subconscious recognizes these intense feelings and plays them back to him. Just like the nightmare, the wish fulfillment dream is just a reflection of the dreamer's emotions. He has a strong and unfulfilled desire.

Any strong emotion, whether it is a fear or wish, is potential dream material.

The most common type of wish fulfillment dreams involves love and romance.

THE GIRL OF MY DREAMS
I had a dream that I was hugging and kissing a girl that I like a lot.

I don't need to interpret these dreams because they simply express a wish. Your dreams mirror your emotions. Whatever you feel deeply can become a dream. Some of our strongest emotions are fears, so that is why we have nightmares. Wish fulfillment dreams come from feelings of emptiness and desperation.

Another common one is dreaming about being with a loved one who has passed away. When there is something that you really want that is impossible to obtain, your subconscious is probably going to give it to you in a dream.

We All Dream

Dreaming is necessary for us to live. It is as essential as breathing. Just like breathing, it is controlled by your unconscious and something you don't need to think about—unless you want to (and, there are a lot of reasons to want to). Dreaming helps keep us balanced. It is a way for us to work out some of our fears and unsatisfied desires. Rarely do dreams predict the future. However, they can sometimes help make us ready for what lies ahead.

If someone says they don't have dreams, then they just aren't remembering them. Dreams occur during the Rapid Eye Movement (REM) period of sleep. Depending on how long you sleep, you could have between three and five REM periods throughout the night. In total, we spend more than two hours per night dreaming. In between the REM periods we have non-REM sleep, which is deeper and dream-less. One reason we don't remember dreams is that when the REM period finishes we immediately start drifting into the deeper non-REM sleep. The best time to remember dreams is right after they finish. Once you fall into the deeper sleep periods it is very unlikely that you will remember any dreams that came before.

Remembering Dreams

If you are not remembering your dreams try this:

Adjust your sleep times. An average sleep cycle lasts about 90 to 110 minutes. If you have an alarm that wakes you up in the morning, try setting it ahead or back about maybe 30 minutes. What you are trying to do is wake up during or immediately after your last REM sleep period.

Tell yourself to wake up. REM sleep occurs in the stage 1 phase of sleep. This is the lightest form of sleep, and is close to our waking state. This makes it possible to give yourself a suggestion while you are falling asleep that you will wake up after your dream. As long as you wake up right after the dream, you will remember it.

Write your dreams down. A strange thing happens after we fall asleep. We actually get a form of amnesia that causes us to forget the last few minutes before falling asleep. So, even if you wake up right after a dream and remember it beautifully, you won't remember it in the morning if you fall right back asleep. To get around this, keep a pad and pen on your nightstand so you can write them down immediately.

Read this book. Your subconscious mind is paying attention to everything you do. So, if you read a book like this, you are letting your subconscious know that you want to study and learn from your dreams.

What It Takes To Be A Dream Interpreter

One can describe a dream interpreter as being like a translator of a foreign language. On a subconscious level this is a language we all already understand. But, since the conscious mind hasn't been taught this language, we dismiss most of our dreams as nonsense. Interpreting a symbolic language requires not only the knowledge of the individual symbol meanings, but also the ability to see how the symbols relate to one another to form a message.

Dream symbols are comprised of three types: 1) archetypal; 2) societal; and 3) personal. Archetypal symbols are symbols that have a universal meaning. Some common examples are water (subconscious, emotions), cars (vehicle for our life path), and dogs (lower animal self). There are many of these types of symbols to learn. The most common are presented in this book.

Societal symbols are those that have a common meaning for a large group of people, but not everyone. One example is a character from a television show. This character would have meaning to everyone who watches the show, but not to everyone else who doesn't.

Personal symbols usually have a specific meaning only to the dreamer. Some of these are friends, relatives, and specific places. To interpret these symbols in a dream it helps to know something about the dreamer and what meaning these images could have to them. Although it is helpful to know the person, it is not necessary. A dream interpreter often has to interpret dreams for complete strangers. Two things that help them in this case are dream context and general intuition. Dream context is the general message of the dream. What, in general, is this dream about? By looking first at all the archetypal symbols you can get an idea of the dream context. Knowing the dream context, the dream interpreter then uses intuition to arrive at the specific meaning for the personal symbols.

Chapter 2 – Elements

The most basic archetypal symbols are the four elements of nature: Water, Earth, Air, and Fire. Their standard meanings and interpretations apply for everyone. Archetypal symbols such as these have had meaning for humankind for thousands of years. These four classic elements are part of ancient Hindu, Japanese, Greek and Native American systems of thought.

Water Dreams

Waves, lakes, rivers, oceans, floods... Water dreams are the most common of all dreams. The reason for this is that water represents the emotions of the subconscious. Emotions, we have already seen, are the substance of which dreams are made. Dreaming of calm and clear water is a sign the dreamer's emotions are also calm and clear. Aggressive water, like tidal waves or tsunamis, represent strong emotions, fears, and negative feelings. Dirty water is a sign that the dreamer's emotions are cloudy or unclear.

Rising Water

> *I was trying to help these people escape from rising water. I start helping them across this large bridge that has old steel frame work. Just as I think I can help them, I am transferred to this concrete bridge. The concrete bridge looked like the golden gate bridge, but different. It had all these cables, yet it had two concrete lanes merging at different heights. The other metal bridge was just beside this concrete bridge but much lower. I have never seen a concrete bridge like this before. This bridge was huge.*
>
> *I concentrate on helping these people across this concrete bridge again. Just as I feel I can help them, I am transferred to the steel bridge only to see the water lapping over the top. I yell to everyone to run. I start to run and as I do I find myself*

> on the concrete bridge again. I look down to the steel bridge and all I can see is some of the steel side bit sticking out of the water. I look at the water and it is rising like a large swell. From the speed I calculate I have less than one minute to escape. I cry out in frustration as I am unable to help anyone.

The water represents dreamer's subconscious emotions, which include past memories and fears. The fact that the water is rising means that his fears are getting closer to the surface. A bridge suspended above the water represents the path his life is taking. The water getting closer means he is being increasingly influenced by his emotions. The second bridge represents an alternative path or choice. The message of the dream is that he is being subconsciously driven to make changes in his path for emotional rather than logical reasons.

The other people are all projections of him. When you change paths, you have to change yourself to suit the new path. That means you have to leave behind certain beliefs and personality traits and get ready to adopt new ones. He can't rescue them because they aren't right for him to have in the future on his new path.

STREETS OF WATER

> I recently had a dream where I was trying to reach a destination (in my dream I knew where but when I woke up I didn't). The streets were not streets, but water. Not rushing water but deep still water shaped like roads. There were buildings in the dream and I passed many on the way to my destination. During my travels on the streets of water, I was stopped by a young man and he had various shorts (clothing) and he was explaining to me why he had each of them and what they were for. He then directed me to my destination. Upon reaching my destination I was facing a fogged mirror in which my recently deceased aunt (who was much like a sister to me) was writing messages to me. I could talk to her, but she could only respond by writing in the fogged mirror. In the

dream I could read them, but upon awakening I don't remember what they were.

The buildings in the dream represent other people. The water represents emotions. Travelling on streets of water means that the dreamer is living life very emotionally. She is driven by her feelings and emotions more than logic. This can lead to following the wrong path and getting delayed by distractions. The boy in the dream talking about his shorts represents being distracted. The shorts represent lack of concentration and how she has only been able to stick with something or someone for a short time before moving on.

The foggy mirror means she isn't seeing her life clearly and that her emotions are clouding her thoughts. Her aunt's death is still very upsetting and she misses communicating with her. So, this part of the dream is fulfilling her wish of being able to talk with her. Even though she doesn't remember the words, the message is still contained in the symbols of the dream. The message of this dream is that living her life too emotionally has distracted her from her life path.

Flooded streets is a common dream

STREETS OF DIRTY WATER

> *I had a dream that I was driving and every direction that I was going in was full with dirty water. It was flooding so much and I felt like if the water was about to pull me down. I kept reversing to get to a different direction/ road but everywhere that I turned there was dirty water.*

Since the water in this dream is dirty, the subconscious is filled with negative attitudes and emotions. Fears and negative beliefs are stopping her from making progress in her life. The way to fix this is to take a critical look at the behaviors and attitudes that come from the past. She needs to become consciously aware of the emotions she feels and where they are coming from. Then she needs to change her behaviors by choosing to do what makes the most logical sense instead of what her feelings tell her.

Earth

The element Earth represents our physical selves and environment. The ground beneath our feet represents stability. So an earthquake or cracks in the ground represent fears of physical loss or security.

EARTHQUAKE WARNING
I was sitting with my parents and the rest of my family in the house I grew up. I could almost predict that an earthquake was coming.
I convinced my parents to get out of our house to a clear alley. We managed to escape through a stairway the moment an earthquake occurred. The earthquake was so severe that the ground cracked.

The ground beneath the house where the dreamer grew up represents his "foundation". These are the basic beliefs and attitudes formed from his early life environment. The earthquake means that he is breaking down and rejecting some of the basic beliefs he was taught as a child. There is a sense of urgency in the dream that indicates that he almost doesn't have a choice in the matter. If he wants to live the life he is supposed to, then he needs to eliminate past programming.

WHEELBARROW
I dreamed I was looking down into the wheelbarrow which had (and actually does have) a bit of dirt and stuff in it. In the corner of the barrow were two $2.00 coins - a bit dirty because

> of the dirt in the barrow - sitting beside each other. The Australian $2.00 coins are gold ...and I believe they were in the heads up position.

The coins are in a position where their heads are up. This means "Heads Up" or watch out for something. It is a warning from her dream that something difficult or unpleasant could soon be happening. A wheelbarrow is used to carry things. So this part of the dream is referring to the dirt she carries around. Dirt in this sense is anything that she should get rid of, like garbage. Something she shouldn't be carrying around. The coins are telling you that these things are about to cause you problems. The problems are probably a physical illness, since the dirt also represents the physical plane.

After reading this interpretation, the dreamer verified that she had been fighting an infection for more than two months. She also had problems with chronic pain and had been addicted to pain killers, cigarettes, and alcohol. So, the toxins in her body were represented by the dirt in her wheelbarrow.

SERIAL KILLER

> I dreamed I got off of work and went out the back door. The street was dark but I knew I only had to go to the end of the road and I would be home.
>
> I began walking and suddenly a man was walking behind me....he held up his hands and over them were clear plastic bags....I knew he was the serial killer the town was talking of and he was going to try to kill me by putting a bag over my head.
>
> I didn't know whether to try to run by him back into work or try to make it home....

The person with the bags on their hands doesn't want to get their "hands dirty". Since the dreamer describes them as a serial killer, then they represent the executives who have to lay people off. From this dream it is clear that she fears that she will be affected next.

In a reply to this interpretation, the dreamer mentioned that her husband works for a company where they already had numerous layoffs and there was a high likelihood of more to come.

Air

The element Air represents the mental plane. So, dreams about air represent our thoughts and plans. In these dreams our more logical side meets our emotions.

CLOUD ANIMALS
In my dream I saw a dark sky maybe clouds then white clouds appeared in the shapes of huge animals.

Clouds are the way we see the element Air in our dreams. The clouds represent the dreamer's thoughts. Animals represent our lower selves, our instincts, and our more primal nature. Since the clouds are in the shape of animals, this indicates that the dreamer is focusing on trivial or unimportant things to satisfy their lower self. The message of the dream is to stop being distracted and to focus on things that have importance, like trying to achieve something worthwhile in this lifetime.

TORNADO
I had a dream that I saw my dad standing over me with my little girl and they tried to tell me something. Then I saw a tornado and my dad didn't look too happy.

The dreamer's dad and her daughter represent the lessons she was taught by her dad when she was a child. A tornado represents a need to cleanse her thoughts or change her way of thinking. The dream is saying that she feels that her dad wouldn't be happy about her current way of thinking which is contrary to what she was taught.

Fire

The element Fire can be a creative or a destructive force. Dreams of fire represent a transformation of consciousness usually through some form of awakening or realization.

DOCK ON FIRE

> Very vivid dream that takes place on a beach where a two-story dock structure that is filled with people erupt into flames. Most die and the survivors jump into the water and are horribly burned.

This dream signals a breakthrough in consciousness. Water represents the subconscious and the beach represents the conscious mind. Being at the beach means that the dreamer was standing at the barrier between the conscious and subconscious. The dreamer must have recently realized or discovered something important that broke through the barrier. The destructive power of fire in the dream shows how this realization will be responsible for big changes he will make. The people getting burned represent the affect this change will have on others around him.

HOUSE ON FIRE

> Last night I dreamed that my house was on fire—not this house I live in, some other house I identified as my own. I was standing afar and I saw the flames take over the whole house—totally engulfed. Then I heard the fire engines. Then I entered my home through the kitchen and to my amazement everything was in perfect condition—nothing was harmed and it had been quite a fire.

A house is commonly a symbol for the physical body. In this dream the fire represents purification of the body. Since the dreamer entered the house through the kitchen, the dream seems to be a message to try to eat healthier foods and purify the body on the inside. Nothing was harmed by the fire because the purification process would leave the body in perfect working condition.

DISTANT FIRES

> We were living in a city in a third world country. The streets were narrow and I knew we were there because we didn't speak the language. It was night time. I could see in the distance fire in different areas. The people were told they had to go inside and stay inside. I was very scared. I knew my children were already inside, but I had to take the dog out. My husband yelled for me to get inside because the crimes were starting. He said he had to get to work and that I had to get inside and take cover. I said to him, "but how will I take the dog out?" He had no time to answer. He had to get to work. Then I woke up.

This dream represents the possibility that the dreamer will be moving soon or at least in for some big changes. The dream takes place in a different country because the dreamer feels out of place in her current environment. The fires represent the destruction of her current life environment. Taking the dog out means having to leave your old life even if you don't want to.

In a follow-up, the dreamer wrote that they were a military family that had moved many times and not by their own choice.

Chapter 3 – Dreams in Motion

Life is not about standing still. It is about movement, taking risks, and exploring new possibilities. When we are moving about in our dreams, whether in a car, train, boat or plane, we are dreaming about the general flow and course of our life.

Cars and Driving

Our life path is represented by the roads we drive on in our dreams. A car is the vehicle which carries us down that path. If the car is parked, then we feel our life is at a standstill. If the car is out of control, then we feel our life is out of our control.

Rocks in a Stream

The first part of it that I remember is driving down this road in my town. I'm not sure if I had been down this road before but it looked vaguely familiar—it was a two-lane narrow shoulder road that looked to be in the middle of nowhere but it was actually right in the middle of my town. Then the road merged into two roads, with one curving away in a different direction. We took the road that curved in a different direction and went further into the middle of nowhere to this strange wooded area that I swear I've dreamt about before. We stopped the car and got out and walked around talking and looking at stuff for a little bit.

Then we got to this place that was like a river/stream with a bunch of rocks in it and my mom and I were on a ledge. My dad had showed up on the bunch of rocks and you could see that the rocks jutted into the stream from the land so he walked out there. My mom decided to jump over to him even though it was way too far for anyone to jump. She ended up hitting her head on a rock and passed out. My dad picked her up and we all started running to the car and this girl that was supposed to be

> my sister (I don't have a sister in real life) appeared behind me and it was Kirra from that show Reba.
>
> We got in the car and my dad was driving and I was in the front seat and Kirra was behind me and my mom behind her. I looked out the window for a few seconds and looked back and instead of my mom in the backseat it's a small laptop computer (like a net book). Somehow it doesn't register to me that this is weird - and I tell Kirra to start CPR so she starts doing CPR on the computer. I tell her that "you don't know where she is inside the CD" so she ejects the CD and then I say "but don't break it, it's all we have to remember her by" so Kirra puts the CD back in the computer and starts doing CPR. This is where I woke up.

This dream indicates that life is a bit boring for the dreamer at this time. The road represents the path she is on. She currently feels that her life is going nowhere. In other words, nothing of consequence is really happening. So, in her dream she decides to take a different road (path), which means taking her life in a different direction. The wooded area represents going to a place that is different and strange.

A stream represents the natural flow of life. If you go with the flow, then you follow your life's path and purpose. The rocks represent stationary objects in the stream; not going with the flow. Her father is that part of her that is hesitant to just go with the flow and see where the stream takes her. He represents her more logical or conservative side. Her mother represents the emotional part of her that wants to jump in the stream and see what happens. Since she gets hurt it shows that she has fears that are holding her back.

The "sister" is a representation of the dreamer. She is the part of herself that she wants to keep safe. The CD and the computer represent her "programming". These are the attitudes and fears that she acquired from her parents and others. The message of this dream is that she really wants to make a big change in her life, but doesn't want to go against what she was taught. That is why she tries to save the computer with CPR.

SPEEDING CARS
> *I was in the street. I don't know what type of vehicle, but it was really low to the ground, and it was like the other cars couldn't see me. I was at a red light and all these big rigs started pulling up next to me, veering to the left almost on top of me. I had to lean left to avoid one of them even. Then, the light changed and (this part is hazy), I can't remember if an accident happened ahead of me or what. But all of a sudden we were stopped in an intersection. Then, all of the cars behind me started to pick up speed as if the drivers were running from something. This thing I was in had no top and it was like a wide skateboard. We got off of it (I say we because I was with a dark-haired woman who I knew in the dream). I grabbed her hand and we tried to make it across the lanes of traffic. But by then the sky had turned grayish brown and the cars were like a giant wave headed right for us. Before I woke up I remember diving out of the way to avoid the cars speeding past me from behind.*

The small and uncovered car in this dream shows that the dreamer feels exposed and vulnerable. Compared to the trucks, his car is small and unprotected. The trucks represent other people who have more power than him.

Being stopped at a red light and then at the intersection means that he feels stuck or blocked in his life. The dream is telling him that his fears or lack of confidence are stopping him from progressing in his life.

The cars that are coming at him and passing him by represent the fact that other people are moving forward in their lives while he isn't. The dark haired woman is the vulnerable part of himself that he is trying to protect. The sky goes dark because he is not following the light, which is a metaphor for not following his life purpose. Instead of trying to move forward, he jumps out of the way and avoids being pushed into something he doesn't want to do.

CAR LEAKING FLUID

> *All I remember from my dream is that I was walking on a dark residential street (it was nighttime), towards my parked car. There were other people walking around in the street but they weren't paying any attention to me. As I walked up to my car, I noticed a lot of red fluid pooling around it, and as I dropped to the ground to investigate, I noticed that it was leaking transmission fluid all over the place. It was literally pouring out like crazy, and I was trying to figure out how I could stop it from losing so much fluid. That's really all I remember, I think I woke up after I realized that it was leaking the transmission fluid.*

A car is a vehicle that carries us down our life path. If it is parked, then that means our life has stopped moving forward. The color red as a symbol also means stop. It is common for a dream like this to refer to loss of a job or income, or some other setback in the dreamer's career ambitions.

Trains

We have seen that cars represent the current motion of our life. Trains in dreams extend the view of our life path to our past and future. These dreams let us see the big picture. So instead of just being about recent events, they cover years of our life.

Any dream can easily be about the past. Your subconscious has a full record of your experiences, so you can easily dream about unresolved issues from the past . Normally with dreams of a different time, there are clues to tell you the approximate time in the past. For example, people wearing old clothes, being on a train that moves backward or moves into areas with increasingly older looking towns and buildings, lack of any modern technology, etc.

Even though the dream is about the past, remember that it must be affecting you in the present for you to have dreamt about it.

NYC SUBWAY
> We were in Times Square - New Years Eve - waiting for 'the bullet to drop'....that would be that ball thing that drops on the stroke of midnight. We being - I have no idea. Then I was on the subway (I've not been on a train in years) with the current leader of Australia and a former 'wannabe' leader. Different political parties. They were waffling on and I was just listening. Then I leaned over to the wannabe and said - I have an idea. How about YOU make the flat rate of tax to be 35% and BLAME HIM - pointing to the current leader. Basically - copy him and let him take the blame.

The dreamer is lamenting over the passage of time. New Years is how we mark the progress of time. A bullet is a fast object, so she feels time is passing by too quickly. The subway is a fast vehicle that moves over a track. Train tracks almost universally represent time lines. So this is another symbol for time passing quickly. The bickering leaders represent her disappointment in the way her life has turned out so far. We blame our leaders for things in our society not working out, so in the dream she wants to blame other people for her disappointments in her life and the fact that many years have passed without her accomplishing all she wanted.

TRAIN DREAM
> I had a vivid dream of a train on a track, and I saw a man scaling the train, and going thru the conductor's window. The man then proceeded to commandeer the train. I don't know where, it was occurring. But I don't think the intentions were good.

Again, the train track represents a timeline. The train moving forward represents moving forward in time. The conductor would be the one responsible for all the passengers, like a political leader.

In this dream the dreamer is hoping for a sudden change in leadership in the near future.

Planes

Planes are vehicles that travel through the element Air. So, they represent our thoughts, projects, and plans. A plane crash is the most common dream involving planes. This represents the crashing of one's plans or projects.

AIRPLANE BUMPER CARS
> I had a vivid dream last night that some people had broken into the computer system of all air traffic controllers, shut them all down and planes were virtually flying into each other and crashing. These men were doing all this from some island and laughing like it was a game.

This dream represents mental confusion. The planes are thoughts and the air traffic controllers represent controlling one's thoughts. So, the dream is telling the dreamer to work on eliminating confusing or distracting thoughts through focus and control. The men on the island represent letting her emotions be in control.

EMERGENCY LANDING
> I dreamt there were storms somewhere maybe in Europe as I was driving on the right hand side lanes. There was a very large motorway, which I think had four lanes. I drove past what was a terrible scene of an accident. Quite a few cars were damaged and lying upside down on the road. I then heard that a plane had crashed there due to bad weather and had landed on this motorway causing all these car crashes. There were road signs and I remember looking at them but it is now frustrating me as I can't remember what they said!! I just remember saying that I hope things are ok by Monday as I will be flying that day myself.

In this dream, the dreamer is driving, so this is about movement on her life path. Other people's cars represent other people's life paths. Driving on the right means she is trying to follow the "right" path. The four lane highway means that things normally move along quickly. However, the plane crash represents the crashing of her plans. This is probably referring to career problems due to a bad economy or job market. It is important to note that the crash had affected a lot of other people, but hadn't affected her yet. So, it shows she is worried about her job or career, but nothing bad has happened yet.

Boats

Because dreams reflect our emotions, and emotions are represented by water, boat dreams, where the dreamer is travelling on water, are very common.

THE PADDLE BOAT
> *I was on an old fashion paddle boat going north on a river, like the Mississippi. The day was bright and warm. The boat was white with steam stacks and large red wheel in the back. I was standing on the top deck and looking up to the sky.*
>
> *Red globe like objects were being catapulted over head. But I couldn't tell where they were coming from. I couldn't see any land. As we went further north the red globes came closer to the boat. One finally hit the big wheel on the back and damaged it.*
>
> *At that point the boat turned back around to get away from the danger but the globes kept coming...but none hit the boat. Though nothing else happened I found the dream kind of strange.*

Rivers and streams represent the flow of life. Going up river, means not "going with the flow", or in other words, not taking the more natural path. In this dream the color red means stop. So, the dream is telling her to stop and turn around. Apparently there is something she is trying to do which is unnecessarily difficult and should be abandoned or done in a more typical fashion. The dreamer's response to this interpretation was simply, "ah, my life in general."

BOAT ON MURKY WATER

> My granddaughter had a dream that she saw me, my husband and two children on a boat and the water was really murky but she could not reach us.

A boat on water represents her current emotional state. When the water is murky or dirty, it means that her emotions are negative, such as sadness or loneliness. The fact she can't get to her grandparents on the boat means that she if feeling emotionally disconnected from her family. It appears that she has some feelings she needs to express but feels unable.

CHAPTER 4 – DREAMING IN COLOR

Colors are archetypal symbols and, as such, have very similar meanings for all dreamers. The meanings for colors in dreams originated over four thousand years ago as part of ancient Hindu philosophy. According to traditional Indian medicine, there are seven energy centers, known as "chakras" that connect the physical body to one's emotional self. Each chakra is associated with a color and certain emotions.

Seven Chakras of Hindu Philosophy

Red

Red is the color associated with the first chakra which is located at the base of the spine. It represents our attachment to the physical world. Red in our dreams is often associated with blood, so it can represent physical vitality or heredity. A dark red, like burgundy is associated with wealth. Since red is also associated with a stop light, it can also be a sign to stop what one is doing.

RED FLUID

> Two nights I have dreamed of a girl I went to high school with. I see her as a child with me and grown up too. She has very light skin, blonde hair blue eyes and her name is Kim. I think she is telling me something but I can't remember. When I wake up, however, I remember last night being in a factory and red fluid or gook maybe even fuel all over the floor,(she was there too). People were dying from it like it was a plague or something (and she was dying too) but someone told me I wasn't going to die because it didn't get on me??? I was walking through the mess in my dream???

This is a dream about friendships from the dreamer's past. The fact that the girl is a child and then a grownup means that this is about behavior that has gone on for some time. Factories are where things are made. So, the girl in this dream represents someone the dreamer knows who is in trouble or having some sort of problem that is of their own making. The red fluid represents their suffering (think blood, pain, etc.). The dream is about the dreamer walking away so she doesn't get hurt too, or have to feel their pain. The dream is therefore about relationships or friendships that the dreamer has walked away from when they became difficult.

RED LOTTERY TICKETS

> In my dream there was man who I was friends with (not someone I know in real life, but in the dream he was obviously my friend) and he was sort of upset because a very good friend of his had won a big lottery, but did not give him money but

actually gave him hundreds of scratch lottery tickets instead. They looked red, almost like the Christmas lottery tickets. And I was trying to comfort him and offered to help him scratch all those lottery tickets and tried to cheer him up by saying that perhaps he would win some money off of them!

There is an important lesson about abundance in this dream. The lottery tickets are red because the color red means stop. So, the dream is telling the dreamer to stop her behavior and attitudes about money. When other people do well she should be happy for them and not jealous. The dream is warning her against being envious of those who succeed or seem lucky. She needs to realize that when you abandon these attitudes and replace them with genuine happiness for the success of others then she will have greater success herself.

TREASURE FIND

I was somewhere near a cave or what later became a cave and we found an entrance, I think we even blew some holes in the wall (When I say "we" I can't recall who else, just sensing 'others'".

Anyway we found something and it was that feeling of when you have discovered something no one else has and I first thought that a large treasure trove of gold had been found but it turned out to be some other treasure. EUREKA!

So I went into the cave expecting to find lots of gold coins or gold statues or just anything gold.

When I walked into the cave I first saw a running fountain, which surprised me and was really nice from what I remember. It had a nice light blue color to it. Then I noticed a giant ring on a cave like shelf, this ring was huge and would slide over someone's head but not over their shoulders.

The ring was not gold or silver from what I recall, maybe a burgundy color, I am not sure, and had a square, or rectangle top where the diamond would go but that was the burgundy color, I don't think it was black but it might have been. It all had an Aztec feel to it as well, maybe Mayan; just a hint of South American flavor is what I recall.

Going into a cave means going into the unknown. The dreamer is probably about to start something new (perhaps a job or business); the outcome of which is uncertain. He expects to find treasure in the cave, so he is hopeful that the risk he is about to take will pay off.

The real treasure he will find is faith. The running fountain is the flow of energy. The ring that goes around his neck is a symbol of power and the burgundy color is associated with wealth. The message of the dream is faith will provide him with the success he wants.

Orange

The color orange is associated with the second chakra which is located near the lower abdomen. Orange in a dream usually represents creativity, sexuality, and reproduction.

ORANGE ROAD

I had a dream that I was driving down a fractured and difficult road called "The Orange Road." Some of the large fissures in the pavement were filled in with orange panels of some kind, like a hasty repair had been attempted. Orange traffic cones and orange road construction barrels were seemingly everywhere.

I'm not sure where I was heading, but in the dream an inner voice told me to follow "The Orange Road."

I was in a small car. It was dark. The pavement was wet. I had to swerve and dodge obstacles as I drove.

The road represents the path the dreamer is taking in his life. An orange road would represent a path filled with creativity. Since the cracks in the road are filled with orange panels it would seem that creativity is a part, but only a part, of his life right now. The orange barrels and cones that he is passing represent the creative opportunities he isn't taking or doesn't have the time to take. The obstacles are the difficulties on his current path. The fact that the pavement is wet means it may become increasingly difficult for him to continue on this path.

So, the dream illustrates a desire for more creative opportunities in his life and career.

OUT OF BODY

> I saw a strange man creature staring at my husband then he changes into a woman in a white dress. The room becomes a white cave. The woman begins to move and the room begins to strobe. I then feel like my body exploded and I was in an orange cloud strange as this sounds I remember seeing myself on the bed and myself floating above and something holding my ankles to keep me there. I somehow did away with this image and got up for a while. When I did relax again I heard what sounded like thousands of rubber bands snapping then I was engulfed in a very, very strong wind. I was going to ride this out until the pressure began to painfully increase I would love to hear any and all thoughts. I can't seem to let this go.

The dream is dreaming about the dreamer's sexuality. The man beast represents aggressive masculine sexual energy. The white woman represents pure passive femininity. The white cave is her womb. The orange cloud represents her second chakra. Some women describe orgasms as a sensation of leaving their body, which is what she describes. Perhaps she dreamt about it in order to help bring balance to her sex life or attitudes about sex.

In the second dream, the snapping sound is a release. And the wind is a loss of sense of security. So, together with the first dream, it seems she has been a little tight regarding sex since it requires her to release and trust.

Yellow

The color yellow is assigned to the third chakra located at the solar plexus. It represents personal power in relation to other people and the ability to direct one's own life.

DARK ANGEL
> Right before I woke up I dreamt that I saw a dark gray or black angel holding a yellow flower. I seemed to be getting closer to it, kind of like zooming in on it with a video camera. As I got closer and closer to it I could see the wings start to spread open. I was looking at the angel from the side.

A dark angel would represent temptation. It appears to be tempting the dreamer with power. Yellow is the color of power. This is a warning that they may be considering compromising their principles or not listening to their conscience in order to achieve greater power or authority.

WRAPPED IN YELLOW
> I dreamt that a co worker of mine wrapped me in a piece of yellow cloth and sent me away. I realized I had a scrubbing brush in my right hand. I was then escorted to an open savannah by a man wearing a tie; I had to get in a section according to the color I was wearing. There were many other people dressed in different colors they were celebrating being promoted and we were told to dance.

Since yellow is the color of power, being wrapped in power by her co-worker means that she has been hoping for a promotion or more responsibility. The scrubbing brush means that up to that point she felt she had been doing only menial tasks. Being sorted by color means she was dreaming of being selected for a position of power.

Green / Pink

Green and pink are associated with the fourth chakra located at the center of the chest. It is associated with love and compassion. Since green is also associated with the green light of a traffic light, it can also mean that it is time to get your life going.

WIFELY DUTIES
> I had a dream that I was at my childhood home with women I don't know. A little boy was injured and I took him and laid him out on the sofa underneath some pillows to support his neck. Next thing I remember was being with that little boy shopping for clothes. The store was dark and no one was there. I saw a man crouching underneath a rack of clothes. I took the boy and began to leave, as I was leaving the store became a church and I saw a priest on my way out. The priest looked at me and said something had been "reneged". The priest's face was flushed and he looked stressed. His eyes were big and light green in color. There was a man standing there with myself and the priest, who pointed out his new shoes.

In this dream the dreamer is reflecting upon her relationships with men (husband, boyfriend, etc.). The injured boy in her childhood home shows that according to her upbringing she feels obligated to take care of men. This obligation means she must take over as their new mother. This includes picking out their clothes, etc.

However, the clothes store being dark and the man under the rack shows she is getting frustrated with this idea. This is contrary to what she was taught to believe. The priest is a symbol for these taught beliefs. What has been "reneged" is her attitude about her duties as a woman. The man with the new shoes means she feels men should get out and do their own shopping and take care of themselves.

Stuck in Throat

> I have a recurring dream in which I am pulling pink or green gum out of my throat. I keep pulling and pulling but it never ends.

The dreamer's throat represents communication. The gum would mean that something is stuck in her throat, in other words, something she is unable to say. Since the gum is green or pink, this means she is having difficulty expressing feelings of love.

Green Water

> I had a dream that seemed to be a warning about an upcoming earthquake. I was standing near a stream/small river/canal. There were numerous oil wells in the area.
>
> I was speaking to somebody about oil wells, and they pointed to the middle of the water and said that's where my oil well was.
>
> Suddenly, the ground lurched up and down. It felt like it had rose up about a foot high, and then dropped. I've never felt an earthquake first hand, so I don't know if that is accurate as to what it would be like in real life.
>
> It seemed like there were only a couple of these jolts, and I was able to get to my feet. In the middle of the water, gas and oil were welling up, as if a well had been uncapped and was now a gusher, or else a pipeline underwater had broken.
>
> The water was not clear blue water, but had a greenish tint to start with. It was about the width of the river along the Riverwalk in San Antonio, TX, but the area had taller grass and was much less urbanized.

> *I woke up after seeing the oil and gas bubbling up and polluting the water.*

The river represents the flow of emotions. The water is green because it has to do with love and relationships. The oil beneath the river represents deeply buried and extremely negative emotional experiences from a long time ago. The ground jolting represents a sudden and surprising event that is causing these buried emotions to resurface. Since there is more than one jolt, it could be that a series of events is the trigger.

IRISH CLUB BAND

> *It was a late summer or early fall afternoon and I was scheduled to perform that evening with a band I have played with earlier this year. It was an Irish club/bar located near where I use to live only a year ago. This club doesn't exist but I noticed that the sign was green and white in a design like a baseball jersey tail. In my mind there was a name, but I don't remember. It was on a large boulevard with angled parking and meters. I was in my car which looked like it was 10 years old, and I don't own a car now and it didn't look like a car I have owned. My ex-girlfriend walks up to the car and tells me she is going to another restaurant on the block until the show. When I walked into the club, I noticed that the sun was very strong and the place was bright and dusty. Only one man was there and he was on the stage with sound equipment. The bar, chairs and tables were all wood and the ceiling was high with round chandeliers. After a few minutes the lead singer of the band arrives. This is where the dream ends.*

Even when we don't own a car, a car in our dream symbolizes our movement on our life path. The parking spots and meters mean that his life (probably music career) has been on hold for awhile. And while he has been parked, he has been burning through money. The green sign means that he has a green light and needs to get moving again. So, this means he feels that his career may start picking up very soon. The ex-girlfriend just represents a time in the past when he was more hopeful about his career. Her presence in the dream means that hope is returning. The bright sun means the spotlight is on him and the dust is another reference to the past and how things will start picking up again. The lead singer arriving means that all the pieces are coming together.

Blue

The color blue is associated with the fifth chakra, located at the throat. Blue represents communication and the ability to express oneself.

BLUE SNAKE

> *In my dream I'm walking somewhere with a cousin or someone and I see 2 dogs and chase them away. Then I turn around leaving the individual I was with and saw a blue snake in the road and hit him with my backpack. Then his owner called the snake "Billy" and the snake turned towards him, hopping and barking. Then the owner came to where I live and threw the snake on me and laughed about it....*

The two dogs represent two people who are behaving like animals. The snake represents deception and the color blue represents communication. This dream means that the subconscious believes that someone is spreading lies or rumors about them. The name "Billy" probably represents that this person is behaving like a bully.

Purple

What people normally refer to as the color purple can vary from a dark indigo to a bright violet. The indigo color, a combination of blue and violet, is associated with the sixth chakra, located at the center of the forehead. The indigo colored sixth chakra is also referred to as the "third eye". It represents our inner vision, thoughts, imagination, and psychic abilities.

ANGRY SPIRIT
> *This was a lucid dream of me being chased by a glowing orb or spirit. I was in a school or a place that had a shower room and this spirit kept appearing at the top of the ceiling in a really bright fluorescent purple glow. It was an angry spirit, female I believe, that was upset with my relationship with my partner. I told it to go back to where it came from, but It took me several tries before it would come out of my mouth, I was extremely frightened. My partner woke me up because I was mumbling and tossing. I hope to never have that dream again!*

Being back in a school often means that the dream contains an important lesson or message. A shower represents cleansing one's self. In other words, getting rid of something the dreamer doesn't need or shouldn't have. The purple glow would represent a part of the dreamer herself. It represents what her intuition is telling her. Since the spirit in this purple glow was angry, this suggests that the dreamer is not following what she believes to be the proper course for her life. The focus of the spirit's anger is the dreamer's partner, so this dream would indicate that some part of her does not believe that this is the right relationship for her. She has trouble telling it to go away, because she knows that what she is seeing is the truth.

White

White and violet are associated with the seventh chakra, located at the top of the head, which is our spiritual connection with God. Dreams with this color usually are about our spiritual purpose. White can also be a symbol for purity or positive energy.

BABY WITH A SCRATCH
> *"I was walking on a sidewalk and came across some people I knew. I stopped to speak to them, as they were having a picnic. There was a baby at this picnic, which I picked up and continued walking on the sidewalk.*

> *This infant started crying, so I pulled her closer. She really seemed to be in some sort of pain, so I started checking her hands and such. I moved her shirt to the side and found what appeared to be like a fingernail scratch. This scratch had scabbed over and the scab was starting to pull away from her back. I kept rubbing at this scab, hoping to give this baby some sort of relief. The scab came off and she stopped crying.*
>
> *From here, I was in a lingerie store. A woman had called and was looking for some sort of white, flowing sundress. The dress was found and the sales associates were passing it to the front of the store. The dress was passed to me and I tried it on. I then awoke.*
>
> *The baby was also wearing like a little white crochet sweater on top of a white onesy."*

The baby represents innocence and the white clothes represent purity. With this in mind, the dream represents the dreamer's own purity and innocence. On the outside, she wears white clothes because she wants to project an image of purity and innocence. However, there is something from her past that she feels ashamed or guilty about, and it has left a scar on her psyche. No matter how innocent she tries to pretend to be, she can't escape this past memory. In the dream she tries to regain her purity and innocence by massaging off the scar. This dream is a message for her to confront her negative feelings and do what she must to forgive the past.

Playing Alone

> *In my dream I was sitting in a regular sized room with no windows and a closed door. The room was completely white with a bright light above me. In the room I was playing monopoly all night with myself I had two little game pieces. Every time I passed Go I was not given my 200 dollars. After a while I felt like I was getting bored of the game.*

Monopoly represents the pursuit of material wealth. It also shows that the dreamer sees life as a game that is getting a bit tedious and he is getting tired of the materialism around him. The bright light above represents the white light of the crown chakra. The focus of the light is for the dreamer to stop concentrating on the material and physical and start looking upward to find his spiritual purpose.

Black and White

The colors black and white often appear together in dreams to represent opposing energies. While white represents positive energy and our highest, best selves, black represents negativity and our lower selves. These dreams usually mean that we are trying to find a balance between two opposing positions. We are trying to settle an internal conflict or struggle, but we have only been able to see things one way or the other. We are seeking balance and perhaps a middle ground, or compromised solution. These are some of the most important dreams we have, so it is important to look carefully to find the symbols containing black and white duality. Some examples are the white and black stripes of a white tiger, or a white bird and a black cloud.

BLACK AND WHITE

> *Dream sequence #1: I'm checking in at a hotel that I used to work at and while I am in line this Swedish woman (I don't know why she was Swedish in my dream) started making unprovoked derogatory comments about black people. How black people were bad and nasty and were not worth the ground that she walked on. I stepped up to the counter and looked at her and said, "Did you say what I think you just said?" She looked me dead in the eye and said, "What, do you have a problem with it?"*
>
> *The desk clerk told me not to worry and that we would fill out a report and turn her into the manager. Apparently the woman worked there. So I check in, but my room isn't ready yet. The desk clerk hands me this long form to sign at the*

bottom and then gives it to me. I guess this was the form to turn into the manager but there was nothing on it. So I take the form and go back outside to where my mother is waiting in the car and we go home to wait on the room.

Dream sequence #2: I get home and go to my bedroom and decide to take a nap. When I wake up my arms are covered with red splotches like I'm allergic to something and then these big purple welts start to appear. I'm screaming that I need to go to the emergency room and my mother looks at me and says that I don't, that I am just over-reacting. My little sister is upset that I am not going to the emergency room and comes to hug me. I am mad at my mother and so I decide that I am taking my sisters back to the hotel with me.

Dream sequence #3: I go back to the hotel but my mom is in the car with me and not my sisters. I leave her in the car again and go in to get the keys to our room. I walk in and go to the desk but the room still isn't ready and it's been about five hours since I first checked in to the hotel. I go in search of the manager about the crazy Swedish woman but keep getting the runaround. I am looking for people that I used to work with at the hotel but having no luck, but I know they still work there. Anyway, I leave and go back to the car and my car and my mother are nowhere to be found.

Of course I wake up before there is a resolution to anything and I am sure that I have left things out but you have the essence of the craziness. In the midst of this I wake up to my bed soaking wet from night sweats.

The first part is about seeing things as only black and white. The black and white duality is represented by people of different skin color, but the symbolism of the dream refers to broader issues and areas of disagreement. In other words, the dreamer has not being able to find a middle ground, or compromise, between two opposing viewpoints. The room isn't ready yet, because she has not been able to resolve this conflict. The form is blank because she doesn't have a solution. Waiting in the car, her mother is in the dream to represent the part of her that wants to avoid conflict. Her sisters are more like her, so that is why she wants them with her.

The second part of the dream shows that she disapproves of an attitude that just wants to end a conflict at any cost. This could mean compromising more than the other person. The mother represents that attitude and that is why she gets angry with her. In the dream the mother downplays her situation, probably because in real life she would just want her to give in.

The third part of the dream is just an extension of the first, to show her that this conflict has been going on for too long. Her mother and the car are missing because this conflict has begun to consume her life.

Chapter 5 – Who Are These People And Why Are They In My Dream?

People are the most common dream symbols. To discover the meaning of people in our dreams it is important to keep in mind that every dream is actually about the dreamer themselves. So, the other people in our dreams usually represent something specific about the dreamer.

It is a common mistake to think that if you dream about someone you know then you must have received a message on their behalf that you are supposed to give to them. Dreams are strictly a personal experience. Everyone has their own dreams and they receive their own messages. That doesn't mean you can't share something you learned in a dream, but it does mean that you shouldn't ignore the message of the dream because you think it is meant for someone else.

Family members often appear in dreams because of our close relationship with them. They most often represent different aspects of our own personality. More often than not, when you dream about your sister or brother, you should interpret their presence as another you. Your parents usually represent the parts of them that you retain inside of yourself. They probably are in the dream to remind you of what they taught you and how you are behaving that is like them or what they would want.

Our biggest nightmares are something bad happening to our loved ones. These probably aren't warnings or predictions. They are just our fears being expressed through our dreams. The dream is not saying whether or not these things will happen. Having a dream like this just means you have a concern that they might. It's up to you to decide if you should act upon these fears.

Very often a familiar person will be in our dream to represent a particular attitude or issue. They may be in the dream because you would expect them to behave a certain way, given the context of the dream. For example, you probably can think of people who would represent the peacemaker, the hot head, or the couch potato. This gives your dream a way to illustrate various choices for behavior that you currently have.

Strangers often are wearing a uniform or possess some other obvious feature that lets us know what they may represent. For example, police may represent protection, discipline, or authority. A doctor could represent advice you have been receiving.

Pregnancy

People in our dream are all ages and types from the fetus to the elderly. Being pregnant in a dream means that there is a potential for you to make a change in your life.

PREGNANT

> I've been having a dream that I'm in a house and I'm holding a baby boy and I turn around and there is a little girl standing behind me and I look down the baby boy is gone and I'm pregnant. What could this mean? I have had this dream over and over again.

Someone standing behind you in a dream usually represents the past. The little girl standing behind the dreamer represents her child-self. The baby boy represents what she has made of her life to this point. The boy disappears because the little girl in her wants her life to be different. A part of the dreamer's subconscious is disappointed that she has not fulfilled her childhood dreams. Being pregnant means that she has the potential to make a significant change in her life and give birth to a new self.

Chapter 5 – Who Are These People And Why Are They In My Dream?

OUT OF THE WOMB
> *I was talking with two women, one who was pregnant. We were just talking and then noticed that the woman's baby was out of the womb, swinging on its cord like it was a swing set, blowing bubbles. We all thought it was cute. Then I realized that this wasn't supposed to be happening and asked the woman if she was sure her baby was suppose to be out when obviously it was still just a fetus. The woman began to be worried and put the baby back in...well through her mouth. I watched her with worry on her face as she put the baby back down hoping it was going back to where it needed to be.*

This means that the dreamer is dealing with something that is premature. The baby being out of the womb means that she is being presented with something before it is ready and perhaps is feeling pressured or rushed to do something too soon. Putting the baby back in through the mouth means this could have to do with something being spoken or communicated.

Babies

Babies in dreams can represent a few different things depending upon the context. They often represent innocence, and in these dreams the dreamer could be lamenting their lost innocence. For some people they represent a new responsibility.

A BABY
> *There was this baby. It was in like a rundown house and being looked after by this old lady. The lady looked like someone out of a witch's tale. Seemed polite and nice but you can see in the eyes there is something else to it. She was Russian, so I couldn't understand what she was saying. She had a baby. And someone was translating for me. There were others there but no one would take the baby. It had like a really demonic name. I was very lucid and I remember thinking in the dream, this is something out of a dark horror movie. Anyway, in the end this woman was getting stressed, so I took the baby in my arms, it*

> *was a sweet little thing, it sort of looked up at me, and then I woke up*

The baby in this dream represents responsibility. So, the dream is about taking on a responsibility that no one else wants. However the horror movie reference means that the dreamer has fears about doing so. The old house and the old lady means that this responsibility is not currently being done properly, and that he feels that he is the only one who can take it on. A Russian usually means that there is a rush (rushing) or urgency to this dream.

Children

Children can represent potential. They often appear in dreams to remind us of the hopes and dreams of our childhood.

TWENTY-SEVEN CHILDREN

> *I was back in school days and walking to school when I walked past my favorite house on the block, a mansion with the most beautiful looking garden. I see a lot of school kids waiting in the garden.*
>
> *A girl comes up to me and asks, "Would you like a lift to school?"*
>
> *"Sure, is the bus picking us up here?"*
>
> *"No, our mum is driving us"*
>
> *"You're all brothers and sisters? How many of you are there?"*
>
> *"27"*
>
> *And as this goes on, I somehow know the elderly couple who have these 27 children, but I only knew them only to have 2 children up until this moment.*

"I had no idea you had 27 kids, I thought you had two", I said to them.
"Oh ", they laughed. It was all so peculiar.

So I peeped into their house to check out how 29 people could live inside this house... It was a mansion, yes, but on the inside it seemed smaller, like a terrace house, like there must've been secret rooms?

I start pushing walls to find secret doors and I find one behind another door. As I swing the door open I see a small room with a shoe rack and flight of stairs (to other rooms) and cockroaches are crawling all up the walls, it was the filthiest section of the house and I start to get a picture of how 25 of their children are treated.

I walk up to the bedrooms to find 2 bedrooms. There are no beds only blankets on the floor. Like orphans, these parents didn't care for these 25 at all. They didn't do their washing or clean their section of the house or talk to them about problems or anything. They were abandoned. Treated terribly and used to it. Still, there were cockroaches everywhere. The other 2 children were treated well by their parents with nice proper bedrooms in the visible sections of the house.

And suddenly the mother comes into the secret room with a bus (somehow my dream allowed a bus to fit inside a house!) I looked at her and she knew she treated these children badly and they deserved more. But like an unintelligent person, she turned to the children and screamed "well none of you have to live here. I saw an ad for places to rent around here you can all move out when you want to" - the children are silent. And I stand there in disgust.

In the next scene, I have of water and detergent. I and four of the children start cleaning the rooms (most of them seem not to understand the situation). I start with the first room near the staircase... I tell the children that they don't have to treat themselves badly because their parents treat them badly. I gave them a plan to live by and how to get money from the government to live. They do not want to move. So we make the place better. I said ignore them and you will have freedom to look after yourselves. You are brothers and sisters you need to be there for each other you are not alone.

I spoke to the parents, "Why do you treat these two nicely and the others not?"

"Well I don't know why we treat Hannah nicely" one of them said to the other and they laugh.

"What do you mean?"

The mother said "Well one day a lady said Hannah was really gifted and we believed she might be as she got older. But she's shown no promise to us yet and probably never will"

"What's that got to do with anything? You were hoping she'd make you both some money?"

"Yea"

Then the other daughters walked in. "DAD! I told you NOT to move my silk scarf from my door! Why'd you move it?" something ridiculous like that. And the parents were really nice to this daughter.... meanwhile I'm thinking (be quiet little girl or they might toss you to the side like the others...you are very lucky) - that doesn't make sense why I would think that. She's not lucky at all. Her parents were crazy.

It is clear from this dream that the dreamer is a person with many talents. Each of her talents has great potential.

The house represents her mind. In her mind she lives with 27 children. And each of these children represents something different she could have chosen to do with her life. The ones that live in the bad sections of the house are the paths she chose to neglect up until now. Only two, did she consider as things worth pursuing.

As a person with many natural abilities, it is difficult to focus on certain ones because it feels like she is neglecting big parts of herself. Thus, most of the children in her dream are neglected. This creates an underlying sadness that will stay with her until she finds a way to express these other parts, or else become satisfied that she doesn't really ever want to pursue them.

ROADBLOCK
> *Last night I had a dream of being outside in a neighborhood and seeing a little girl (3 or 4 years old) running away through the neighborhood towards a busy street. Her older sister (I think) was chasing her trying to stop her. Their mom was not aware of what was going on. As soon as the little girl was getting close to the busy street, a wall of people, cars, debris came through (like a tsunami....but no water). It was like a river coming through and I was standing in the sidelines, not running from it...like this tsunami of people/debris just flowed right in front of me then stopped. I was then worried about the little girl and if she survived.*

The little girl represents the dreamer as a child—full of hope and ambition—anything is possible. The older sister represents the more "mature" self—the person who is more "realistic" and more willing to settle for the ordinary rather than go for an impossible dream. When the little girl gets to the road the debris blocks it up. This means she is blocked from fulfilling her dreams. The dreamer wonders if the little girl survived because she wonders if that little child that once believed she could accomplish anything is still inside of her.

Boss / Co-Workers

Okay, after working a long day and putting up with office politics, big egos, and backstabbing, these may be the last people you want to show up in your dreams. However, dreams about people from the office can really help you understand your goals, ambitions, and general satisfaction with your life.

THE BOSS AND A RING

> I had a dream that I was with my boss and we were standing side by side, our shoulders touching. We exchanged a bag of tea.
>
> Another dream was that I was with my co-worker who has been at the company for many years and who has power with the higher ups. In the dream, we were looking at jewelry. She was criticizing all of it. She slipped a rare very beautiful ring on my ring finger. The ring was not big or gaudy, just tastefully done and with plenty of sparkle and class. She was trying to sell or auction the ring. The ring stopped at my knuckle and didn't go further.

The first dream means that the dreamer feels that she is an equal with her boss. In America, a tea bag is a symbol of protest. So, she resents that she is beneath him and thinks that she could do a better job.

The second dream is really part two of the first dream. She is dreaming about her concern for her career. Clearly, she thinks that she deserves a raise and possibly a promotion, which is represented by the ring. The co-worker trying to auction the ring means that perhaps there is a possible opening for a higher position, but since the ring doesn't fit, she is worried that it won't be given to her.

Apparently she was correct about not getting the promotion, because a short while later she lost her job.

REMOTE CONTROL

> A woman I knew as a coworker, and who I have not seen in 5 or 6 years, now lives in the Los Angeles area.

Chapter 5 – Who Are These People And Why Are They In My Dream?

Here is the setting.

It was the middle of the day, and she was approaching her car that was parallel parked along a street. There were large single story industrial/warehouse type buildings along the street. The street was lined with parked cars. My point of view is about in the middle of the street, maybe 50 yards from the point she is crossing the street going to her car.

She unlocks the car with a remote and gets in, but before she starts the car, she is attacked. It was difficult to see details, because of the glare off the rear window, but it looked like a man grabbed her from behind. He had been hiding in the back seat, apparently.

The back door opens on the driver's side (which is also the street side) and a large man with brown hair that is dirty and dressed in a black shirt and black pants gets out. He is laughing.

In the dream, I wonder how he could have hidden in the car, since I assumed it had been locked.

My viewpoint suddenly changes to a face to face position. I do not recognize him, though I know he is a "bad guy."

Without asking he shows me a little metal box in his hand. It is square with a push button and a little square red light.

He pushes the button, which lights the light, and all the car doors along the street unlock at the same time.

He laughs, then opens the rear car door and pulls out an automatic rifle of some kind. I don't know weapons on sight, but I can tell it is a military style machine gun.

He holds it over his head and laughs some more.

> *That is all I can recall now. When I woke up my first thought was to warn this woman about some kind of danger having to do with her car.*
>
> *She probably thinks I am completely nuts, now. Maybe I am.*

In this dream the dreamer mistakenly believes that he has had a dream about someone else. He even contacts her when he wakes up to tell her. It's important to analyze every dream for some personal meaning. Our dreams usually reflect our concerns about what is happening in our own lives and other people in our dreams are usually symbolic.

The reason this woman is in his dream is because she now lives in California. This is what is commonly referred to as the "left" coast because of the liberal thinking that most people that live there share. The car in his dream represents movement of his life. Since the car is parked it would represent that he is concerned that his life could stop moving. The buildings in the dream represent businesses and places of work. By putting the car and building symbols in context it would seem that the dream is trying to represent unemployment.

The remote represents control (ie. remote control). The dream shows the woman using the remote to open her car, showing her controlling where her life is going. Since she symbolizes liberals, it means that the dreamer believes that the liberals have gained control. However, she is attacked by someone who is already controlling everyone's cars. This person in black would represent the government officials and how the dreamer feels they secretly want to take more control of our lives. The gun shows that they have the power to do this.

Although the dream seemed to focus on the former co-worker, the dreamer needed to realize that this dream was a reflection of his own fears about where the country is heading.

Celebrities

Celebrities in our dreams represent our dreams of success. They are the perfect symbol to represent the fame and wealth that eludes most of us.

REALITY STAR
> *I dreamt that my friend left me a message saying that there was some issue at work, that someone was accusing me of throwing away their paperwork. I saw the paperwork outside sitting on a tree. In the dream, I had not done such a thing, and in the next scene I was explaining this to my accuser who happened to be a "celeb-reality" star from a show I watch on TV. Next, I find myself in another room with her (the celeb-reality person) and there is an open closet in front of us, which is well stocked with bottles of cleaning solution. I'm explaining to her that she can use them anytime she wants, to just use them when she needs to clean, and not to wake me up when I'm sleeping. Then I'm in some shopping mall type of place and I'm walking along and someone gives me a book as a gift. She very intensely inserts a bookmark shaped like a horse shoe in the middle of the book. I thank the person and continue on looking around at different things at the mall. I realize later much to my disappointment, that I lost the book and I go back to search for it. I find it after a little inquiry and effort, and then I see some former co-workers gathered around the mall. One of them sort of indicates to me that they don't want to lose a certain person, who we see walking around the mall carrying a child's baby doll.*

The reality show star represents the dreamer's personal fame, i.e., all the people who know her or knows of her, but she doesn't really know well. Being accused of throwing away the paperwork means she is being held responsible for what other people do. So if they do bad work, it impacts her. The paperwork in the tree means that accusations like this can stop her career growth.

So, this dream is about how she thinks she is perceived by others, probably in the work place. The closet of cleaning supplies means she thinks she needs to work hard to keep her reputation clean by defending herself.

Being in the shopping mall represents material success. The horseshoe in the book means that she feels other people may think she got to where she is through dumb luck and not through any special skills or knowledge. Losing the book shows that she doesn't really need luck. But by looking for it and finding it, her dream is revealing that she does believe that they may be partly right.

The co-workers not wanting to lose a person means that she is concerned about layoffs or firings while she continues to enjoy success.

AMBITIONS SHOT DOWN

> *I was in a minivan together with a famous actor. The actor was seated in the passenger side. And I'm seated at the back of the van. In front of us there is another vehicle where a carjack is going-on. Due to traffic, the carjackers got angry and then began shooting at us. The driver and the actors were not shot. But I was hit three times in the upper body, even though I'm trying to avoid the gunshots. Then they brought me to a hospital, but I'm still alive. Then I woke up from that dream.*

When we dream of celebrities we are dreaming about our own ambitions for success. The van represents the movement and progress of this part of the dreamer's life. Since he is not driving, he does not feel in control of his own success. The traffic means he is experiencing a slow down. Getting shot means he is concerned about his ambitions being shot down. This would correspond to an event such as getting a bad performance review.

Hairdressers

It may be hard to believe, but dreams about one's hairdresser are rather common.

> HAIRDRESSER
> With my hairdresser parking my car, an old boyfriend pulls in behind me and gets out of the car the same time we do. He pulls out a very small handgun and starts shooting I'm not hit at first but my hairdresser is and is killed, I'm eventually hit but I can feel the bullets hit my clothes but they don't hurt or penetrate my skin.

The hairdresser represents the dreamer's superficial or outer self. The boyfriend firing at her represents the fact that she feels other people are angry with her. This is probably not just referring to him, but to other people who may feel that she is self-centered or uncaring. The fact that she is dreaming this means a part of her is feeling some guilt for past behavior.

However, since the bullets don't penetrate, she believes that she cannot be hurt by whatever people are thinking about her.

People Who Have Passed Away

"I dream dead people."

It sounds like a line from the movie *Sixth Sense*. But dreams about people who have died are among the most common of all dreams. A large number of these could be classified as wish fulfillment dreams. Sometimes the passing of a loved one leaves us with a profound sense of loss or deep regret. Our wish is to be back with them. But that is not possible in our waking state. So, instead, our subconscious creates this reality in our dreams.

The dream often starts off with a revelation that the deceased person is not really dead. They were simply away on a trip, or hiding somewhere. They behave like everything is normal but the dreamer usually remembers that this person died.

DEAD OR ALIVE?

> My dream is about my father that passed away a couple of months ago. I keep dreaming him being dead and then coming alive and then dead again.

This dream is just to help the dreamer accept her father's passing. Part of her is still in denial.

Here is an example of a dream where the person in the dream is dead, but in real life they are not.

COMMEMORATIVE PLAQUE

> Last night, I dreamt that a girl at my school died. She and I don't talk often, and she's kind of annoying, but I have no reason not to like her. After her death, a sort of plaque was hung up at my school - I guess to alert everyone there of her death. I knew it was hung at school, but the wall looked like a wall in my empty garage, and I can't remember any of the normal signs or clutter that usually fills the garage in the dream. Also, the name on the plaque did not belong to the girl who had died. It was a celebrity with the same name as her, but not her gender and also a different spelling of the name. After I noticed that school looked like my garage, the dead girl appeared and began conversing with me, although I knew for a fact the entire time that she was dead.

This dream is about a change that is occurring in the dreamer's subconscious. The death is not the death of a friend from school. Instead it is about a big shift in her outlook on life. A garage is where she parks her car and stores things. Since the garage is empty it means she has cleaned past attitudes out her subconscious mind. The plaque represents the death of the old person she was and it has replaced her old attitudes, leaving her clean and clear headed. The reason the name on the plaque is a celebrity has to do with her old attitudes about herself. Her childhood wish to be a famous celebrity is being released as she gets ready to focus on a new path for her life. Conversing with the dead girl is the same as talking with her old self. In this case the conversation was about taking that childhood optimism, and faith that she can do anything, and redirecting it to a new plan.

Police / Soldiers

Police in our dreams represent authority or protection. Soldiers usually represent bravery or more oppressive authority.

SISTER GETTING MARRIED
There was no one I knew in the dream but it was supposed to be my sister getting married. (My sister got married a year ago and is expecting a baby now).

In the dream I was in the wedding. But, it wasn't really me in the dream. It starts in a hall that has a red aisle and wooden church like seats. Four people go ahead of me down the aisle. I was standing on the left BUT I was a man in the dream. The woman I was escorting down the aisle was "my wife" (whom I have never seen before). I get to the end of the aisle and the two couples that went before us turned around and were sitting on chairs, looking at me. The woman sends me back up the aisle to find folding chairs for me and her to sit on.

I walk back up the aisle to find the chairs. I find them in a closet and start back down the aisle. When I come back down the aisle I see children sitting around a table looking at coins. I am then pulled into a pew by someone. I look back down the aisle and I see the "bride" standing and facing us where the children were playing with coins on the table. She is not my sister. She has bright red hair and is wearing a striped dress. The ugliest striped dress I have ever seen. The colors were yellow, blue, red and purple. The stripes were horizontal.

I'm telling myself that my sister is pregnant. But this woman just looks a bit fat to me. The woman then starts chanting something incoherent that sounds like the title to a dance. She starts to flap her arms like a chicken.

Then a whole parade of US Marines dressed in blue uniforms with white hats start marching into the room from the other side of the altar. They were 4 men across and 20 men in each row. They march up the aisle along the far wall and then around and back down the center aisle. As they march past me I see a small group of men and boys holding swords up over the marine's heads as they pass. As they march past me they start doing the same "dance" the "bride" was doing. Flapping their arms. They stop and go back and forth like a chorus line. They start singing the chant then continue down the aisle and out the room. A row of chickens then go by.

I look back down to where the "bride" is, and the altar has been transformed into a kitchen. The "bride" is now cooking food for her guest. She is cooking the chickens. The chickens are cut up and being deep fried and roasted in special ovens.

The "bride" is talking while she is cooking but I can't remember what she was talking about. I asked why was the bride cooking for the party, but no one answered.

This is about the dreamer's fears of getting married. The chickens represent being "chicken". The marines represent courage. The confusion with the chairs represents her feeling that weddings can be complicated to plan. The coins represent the cost of the wedding. She is a man in the dream, because her feelings about marriage are more commonly felt by men. Women are "supposed" to be in love with the idea of marrying. Since everyone ends up doing the chicken dance (even the marines) it shows that her fears are strong. The bride cooking the chickens means that eventually she will overcome her fears.

Chapter 5 – Who Are These People And Why Are They In My Dream?

I HATE NAZIS

> The dream I had last night was long. I even awoke, went back to sleep, and it started where it left off. It began with a sense of dread. I was with several people, when who should appear but SS officers and Nazis. I have never dreamt of Nazis. They were moving though the crowd, looking for people. There was a sense that I needed to avoid them. There were scenes of us skirting around them. At some point I was in a large assembly of people. There was a religious feel about it. Everyone was standing and praying. When it ended we left. I noticed every one moving towards the exits. However, a couple of men moved unseen to an out of order restroom. I followed, having a sense that I had to follow. I felt that it was important not to follow the crowd.
>
> Before I entered I noticed two men that were stealing a large traffic sign. I knew this was an act of a small rebellion. The sign was in German. I knew I was in the mountains. The bathroom was old and forgotten. We followed a number of hallways. All dark abandoned areas. Once or twice the windows were broken and the wind was blowing in. We finally entered an area that we knew would be safe. Hidden well below ground, it was empty of furnishings. It was dark. It was safe. Then I awoke the second time.

The Nazis represent authority in its most oppressive sense. Their presence means that the dreamer is trying to avoid oppressive people and situations. In other words, she does not want to have a boss or someone who tells her what to do. The church represents sanctuary; a place where there is no one to boss her around. It also means that she feels the only boss she has to answer to is God. When she leaves she doesn't follow the crowd because she wants to be on her own and do her own thing.

A traffic sign is another symbol for something telling her where to go and making decisions for her. Taking that down means she rejects the notion that she needs to do what she is told. The mountains represents wanting to be more on her own and more independent. The bathroom is another symbol for a place where she can be left alone in privacy. Since it is old and forgotten it means that she hasn't been able to find that solitude in some time.

The hallways and abandoned areas again represent getting back to a past time with less authority and more self direction. Since the windows are broken and air is getting in, it means that other people can still find a way to get to her and find where she has been hiding. She is discovering that being on her own is a tough thing to accomplish. However, at the end of the dream she feels she has accomplished it.

In summary, the dream indicates that the dreamer has a desire to be a very independent person. She wants to think for herself and follow her own path without someone else giving her directions.

KEEPING THE PAST IN THE BASEMENT

In the beginning of this dream there are men chasing after me, I don't know what I've done or why they are looking for me. There is a guy (presumed to be a police officer) he takes me down to the basement of this rather large house, it's about 3 stories high and the basement is below ground. The room that I am led to is in the farthest corner of the house from the entrance. It kind of reminded me of a janitor's closet from a school. There is a TV on, very musty damp smell and a green couch in the room.

The officer instructs me to wait there until it is safe and he will come get me. While I'm sitting on the couch there is a loud noise coming from upstairs. I then hear people start to come down the stairs that lead to where I am, so I hide in a closet that is filled with mops, brooms, and a water heater. This is where I discover another girl and her sister dressed in matching red jump suits with a white stripe down both sides. One of the girls is around 16 while the other 8. The oldest of the girls puts her finger up to her mouth and shushes me.

The men coming down the stairs are bringing the body of the police officer down. He has been badly beaten and there is blood all over the place. They start looking through other closets and under tables, I'm assuming to find us. But one of the guys (he is rather tall and muscular) sits down on the couch and turns the TV to football. Which in turn makes the first guy stop his search and start scolding him for being such an idiot. They then stomp up the stairs and it is very quiet. The 2 girls and I come out of the closet and start to search for a way out. We then discover a set of stairs (kind of like a servant's access to the upper rooms) this takes us to the first floor where the front door is located. Both of the girls manage to make it outside when I hear the men coming. The nearest thing to me is stairs that go up to the second and 3rd floors. I run up them to the top and into the first room on the left.

There is a bed made with white sheets, the window is open blowing the very sheer white curtains in the rainy breeze. The men are coming up the stairs and split, one comes into the room I'm hiding in and the other to the right. When that man comes into the room he stops and looks at me, smiles, and then turns around and walks out the door. My heart begins to pound as I search for a way out, I notice outside the window is a green eve. There is a bar across the window that I grab a hold of and swing myself through the screen in the window. I then begin to go around the house on other eaves, all of them a dark pine green. I find a window that is open and go through it.

In this room is a man laying on a bed. He is wearing a baby blue button up long sleeve shirt, perfect skin. It is my ex-fiancé. I go to sit on the bed beside him and he brushes his hand to my cheek and picks up his phone. He then sends a text message to someone telling them to stop the search. I lay down beside him and he puts his arms around me and covers us up. He then kisses me ever so sweetly, I giggle and made a comment that it had been over 2 years since I'd felt his lips on mine. This makes me cry realizing that my fiancé is back home. Once he falls

> asleep I sneak out of the house for good and start running for home. While I was running I kept thinking to myself how bad my heart hurt. It felt like I had a heavy burden on my chest although I haven't made any contact with my ex for a long time.
>
> It's barely dusk and a light mist of rain is falling. As I'm running I find the girls that were in the closet with me are still in their red jump suits, hiding in plain sight. They begin to run with me....then I woke up.

This dream is about the dreamer's past relationships and how certain things about them she wants to keep secret.

The men chasing her all represent past men in her life. The police officer represents her efforts to keep her secrets safe. The house represents her mind with each floor representing different levels of consciousness. The basement would be the deepest level, so it is the place where she keeps her secrets. The room she is in is farthest from the entrance because that would be the hardest place for someone to get to and find out the secrets about her past.

The TV, green couch and musty smell represent the way she feels about past behavior—basically like a sleazy hotel room. The closet she hides in is where she keeps her past selves. The eight-year-old is her before puberty and the sixteen year old is her post puberty. The red jump suits are probably some type of racing uniform. So, it means she was in a big hurry to grow up.

The police officer getting beaten up means that she believes she will be unable to keep the truth hidden. The guy who turns the TV to football represents the regrets she has over wasting time on men who never cared that much about her. The two girls making it out the front door means she is ready to be more open about her past.

As she goes upstairs she is getting ready to "come out of the closet" and be open about her past and how it affects her in relationships. The bed with the white sheets represents purity in the sense of being able to forgive and erase the past. The rainy breeze is like a shower that washes away past sins. So, when the man sees her there, he just turns around and leaves because she has eliminated the guilt from that relationship.

The green eaves are outside, so they represent physical touch and affection. It seems that once she heals the past she will be more comfortable with physical contact. The man who is her ex-fiancé is wearing blue because blue is the color of communication. So by talking openly about her past, these memories will stop haunting her.

Unfortunately, another part of her begins to surface next. This is the part that is afraid of revealing feelings from the past and shows that she still has some confused emotions. So, as she runs away, she is rejoined by her past selves and back to the way she was before.

Chapter 6 – Animal Dreams

Often we dream of animals because they typify a certain animal-like behavior we are seeing in certain people. The dreams in this chapter use animals to represent behaviors such as dishonesty, deceit, intuition, and aggression.

Dogs Are #1

They live with us. Some even sleep with us and eat off our plates. Their behavior is the most human-like and we treat them like members of the family. So, it's not surprising that dogs are the most common animal appearing in dreams. What is surprising is that, in our dreams, dogs usually represent other people.

Dogs are basically instinct-driven creatures. They behave according to their genetic programming and training. Through positive and negative reinforcement people are able to train dogs into a certain type of behavior. Unlike people, dogs don't have a conscience that tells them right from wrong.

In most dreams, dogs represent the animal-like behavior of people. When people behave like animals we behave selfishly and without concern for other people. We lose control of our emotions, and our fears take over our behavior.

When dogs appear in dreams they represent people who are behaving like animals.

A dog in a dream can represent a person who the dreamer feels cannot be trusted. This is similar to when you meet a strange dog and wonder if he will bite you if you try to pet him.

Thanksgiving is Going to the Dogs

> In a house (not familiar), but was obviously "home" as in where I lived. It was Thanksgiving and people kept arriving at the door. The interesting thing was that each group of people arrived with their pet dog at the door. Each time the dog kept getting larger, so by the end of the dream someone had arrived with a huge great dane type dog. Our house was on the smaller side, and I kept wondering how everyone was going to fit. The tone of the dream was light hearted though and I would almost giggle each time I opened the door and there was a larger dog, but at the same time was thinking why would people bring their dogs unannounced over to our house? I welcomed each new group and dog in and wondered how big the next dog was going to be. People were discussing pie and such... end of dream. Oh also have to mention that my Mom was present and we lost her almost two years ago now to cancer.

Every person that arrives at the door is bringing their lower animal self. So, the dreamer is dreaming about being aware of the general bad behavior, deception and untrustworthiness of others close to her. The dogs get bigger because the longer she waits to say or do something to stop the behavior, the bigger the problem becomes. Since it is Thanksgiving and her mother is in the dream, this likely has to do with a family matter.

Pit Bulls

> Black pit bull dog showing up and trying to attack me and brown pit bull is fighting the black pit bull. Then they both turn on me while attacking my right arm.

There are two people around the dreamer who are fighting a lot, like pit bulls. Their color is a way of identifying who these people are by their skin color. The dream is telling her that she is worried that these two will soon turn their anger onto her.

Chapter 6 – Animal Dreams | 79

Remind you of anyone?

VISCOUS DOG

> I had a dream the other night about a vicious white dog with a red mouth that kept trying to bite and did bite me a few times? He had a hold of my hand and I was trying to fend him off. It was wild!! I was with a woman but I don't know who she was and we were trying to find a way to escape. I was around a Land Rover and I was trying to climb to the top and then tried to get in the car to escape. The lady was trying to help me and escape with me. I managed to get the door open and climb in to get away but then the car drove itself and I kept putting my foot on the brake and it wouldn't stop. I was heading around a very narrow road at the edge of a cliff and as the car was moving around, the road was getting narrower and eventually the car fell. I must have woke from this dream then as I don't remember anything after this, but I remember feeling that I was not in control of any situation and I felt frightened and frustrated.

Most likely, the white dog represents a white woman. The red mouth is the clue that it is a woman because this could represent lipstick. Dogs represent our animal selves. So clearly this is a woman who behaves immorally to say the least. The woman biting and holding onto the dreamer's hand is clearly trying to stop the dreamer from getting what she wants.

The woman she is with by the Land Rover is probably the same woman as the dog. So, the dreamer is seeing two sides of this woman. The side she shows her is the one that pretends to be helpful. However, while she pretends to be helpful she is also sabotaging the dreamer. A car without brakes is a classic representation of sabotage.

In a follow-up message, the dreamer confirmed that there indeed is a woman that she does not know if she should trust.

Cats

Small cats in a dream represent our intuition. If we dream about a cat we are probably suspicious of some secret or deception, but we don't know for sure.

CAT ATTACK

> I dreamt that my boyfriend's 23 year old daughter, who I do not get along with, brought a cat home, and every time I looked at that cat it would attack my arm and I mean put my whole hand down its throat, I would have to beat it off me, the 3rd time it attacked, I could not get it off my arm, so I took it to the bathtub, turned the water on, put my arm in and drowned it.

It is clear that this dream is about the dreamer's relationship with her boyfriend's daughter. The cat represents secrets or things unseen. The dream indicates that she feels that the daughter may be trying to undermine her relationship with her boyfriend by saying things to him when she is not around. By taking the cat to the bathtub she is trying to cleanse herself of the hurt and negativity she is feeling because of her.

Big Cats – Lions and Tigers

Big cats are often associated with feminine personality traits. Sometimes a woman dreaming about a large cat is dreaming about her sexuality and attitudes about sex.

The black and white stripes of a white tiger represent a dual nature or two opposite types of behavior. In the case of tigers, the duality represented is passive versus aggressive sexual behavior. As kings of the jungle, lions are commonly associated with strength.

LIONS OUTSIDE
> I had a dream when I was 14 (now I'm 24), that my family lived in Africa and the house we lived in had a front door that was like a double door that didn't shut all the way. There was a two foot gap between the two doors. At night we had to lock up the house and try to get the doors completely closed because the lions always prowled around our house at night. This one night my kitten was outside so my brother went out to get her. Right then two lions jumped on him and dragged him off and were eating him. Still to this day I remember his screams for help. I then woke up crying and couldn't stop for like an hour.

This dream shows the insecurity the dreamer was feeling at that difficult time in life. Since the doors didn't close on his house, he felt vulnerable and unprotected. Lions represent strength, so he felt weak (like the kitten) compared to the other people around him at the time. His brother simply represents the fears he had about his own security.

LION AT SCHOOL
> I dreamt that a man took me to a school and at the school we walked towards the dorm rooms. When we got to the dorm rooms it was like a house on the campus and the door was open. When we got to the door I looked inside and saw young people only of the white race lounging throughout the house. We walked into the front room and young people were

everywhere with books like they were studying or doing home work. One young man got up to inquire why we were there and the strange man I was with asked for the dean or the person in charge. We were directed to the kitchen.

When we got to the kitchen, which you could see from the front room, I saw adults in the kitchen. As soon as I stepped in the kitchen and saw the dean I turned into a lion. A young but huge full grown lion and I started roaring. I then ran out of the house and then began running all over the campus roaring at every one I saw.

There was a woman in particular I saw and ran up to and I roared at her and she trembled with fear and took her arms to cover her face. I was roaring but I had a joy I felt. Then I looked I saw the dean and another gentleman come out the house with rifles and it was like every time they raised their guns to fire at me they lowered them in tears as though something stopped them from firing. When I saw this as a lion I was deeply moved and ran around one of the school buildings and woke up.

Dreaming about school means that the dream is about an important life lesson. Studying means preparing for what comes next in life. The dorms represent the dreamer's home. The dream seems to be telling her that she is preparing for a life in the home. The man represents a husband and the dean indicates that he will be in charge. So, this indicates that she believes that she will most likely always be a wife that doesn't work outside the home. The kitchen is another symbol that suggests she will be a domestic woman that cooks for the family.

However, the lion indicates that this may not be what she really wants. She fears that she will become one of those angry women who are discontented with domestic duties. She roars at her husband as a way of expressing her discontent. Although this angers him, he doesn't shoot the rifle because he understands her point of view. Just knowing that he understands helps her feel better.

COUGAR

My boys and I were in our apartment and there was a cougar in it too. We were very afraid. At the same time the landlord was sending some guys over to do work on the apartment. As we went from one room to another in fear, the cougar was in an upstairs bedroom. (We actually don't have an upstairs; its one floor). We were in the kitchen and a worker and his crew show up. The head guy knocks on the door to tell us they are here and we have to get out. We exit and my mom is there to pick us up.

My boys' attitudes change when we go outside and my youngest is giving me a hard time because I want so badly to warn the workers about the cougar. The boys say that they need to call Skip Cunningham (a name I don't know put keeps coming up). He catches wildlife animals and sets them free. Finally, I am crying to my mom about my boys and their attitudes and we go to a table in the front yard to tell a woman about the cougar and to call Skip Cunningham. A male worker overhears me and gives me papers to sign.

Since the dreamer never sees the cougar, it represents a hidden fear. A cougar is a stealth predator, so this indicates that she has a fear of something sneaking up on her. In other words, she is worried about something she may not be prepared for. A cougar also represents a single woman, so this could represent her as single woman. Having some work done on the apartment probably means this has something to do with physical changes or improving her physical appearance. Since she has to leave the apartment this could be concerning a loss of home or security.

Since the cougar is upstairs the issue is hanging over her and affecting everything she does. The workers represent someone who is responsible for making these changes happen. This could be the spouse, lawyer, etc. Skip Cunningham probably represents someone who could help her to feel better. Skip Cunningham in real life is an actor, so this could be someone who is only pretending to help. However, most times we remember a name, there is meaning in the name. So, the name, "Skip", could mean skipping out on the relationship. In the dream, "Skip" would set the cougar (the dreamer) free.

The part with her son's attitude represents the concern she has of how the children may be affected. The papers and table in the yard represents some contract or formal document, perhaps divorce papers or similar.

WHITE TIGER

> I dreamt I was at an older house. It seemed familiar to me, possibly my dad's. I went to go inside the house when I noticed there was a huge white tiger sitting on the fence, or perched like a cat is more like it. I wasn't so much fearful as I was worried and curious. I asked my dog to come in the house, since she was curious too, but no. She didn't follow. She walked right up to the big cat and fed it her ice cream cone. And the cat took it and left.
>
> Then once I entered the house, the person I assumed to be my roommate told me that we had guests. I went to greet them, there were 2 men. One of which must not have been that important because I quickly forgot his existence once I saw the second. He was beautiful. I couldn't tell you what color exactly his eyes were, they were like every shade of blue and green imaginable. Very striking. Some time must have passed at this point because it was dark outside, and he was holding me in his arms. He asked me " Have you ever experienced the real moment?" Which made perfect sense to me at the time I suppose, because I replied "No." Then the lights went out, and I woke up."

When you dream about animals you are usually dreaming about your lower self—your animal instincts. In this case the dreamer is dreaming about her romantic and sexual urges.

The tiger represents her femininity. Since tigers are aggressive, it represents potentially being more aggressive in her pursuit of romantic relationships. However, tigers have stripes, which represent duality, or a choice between two approaches. The tiger sitting on the fence means she is undecided about the right choice to make. Since she was worried about the tiger, she is concerned about choosing the correct behavior and approach.

The old house, possibly her dad's, represents her upbringing—what she has been taught about proper behavior toward men. The ice cream cone represents the male genitalia. Dogs are rather simple in nature. They are pretty much satisfied to be fed and pet and given attention. So the dog in the dream represents just wanting to be satisfied. Being fed the ice cream cone means being satisfied sexually.

The two men in the house represent two choices. The first man is just your average guy. Nothing special, but more like the type of guy her father would approve of. The second man represents the ultimate in romance and physical attraction—mysterious and strong. He represents the romantic ideal of someone who sweeps her off her feet.

The only other symbol is the darkness. Darkness means something she doesn't want to be out in the light. In other words, something she would rather keep private.

Birds

We see birds as objects in the sky; the element Air. When we dream about birds we are dreaming about our thoughts; the things that are on our mind.

> THE OWL AND THE CLOUD
> A white owl is flying into a black cloud. When you can't see the owl anymore lightning strikes a pile of sand and lights up a golden shovel. In the background there are shadows that have the shapes of humans.

The owl is white and the cloud is black. This means two opposite view points, or two opposing views coming together. When this happens, the lightning strikes like a flash of genius. It strikes sand and a shovel, which means the ideas are now becoming a reality into some sort of tangible project. The shadows represent all the people who become involved in this project after the compromise is reached.

Mice

Mice represent irrational fears. They symbolize things we are afraid of, but in actuality are too small to hurt us. Rats, however, represent dishonest people.

> MICE
> I had a dream that I walked into my living room and there were holes at the base of the wall, then I saw mice running back into the holes. My roommate and I were just standing there then I woke up.

The mice represent things that the dreamer is afraid of, but shouldn't be. The walls represent the boundaries between her and others. Since the mice are in the walls this means that she probably has some fear of intimacy or getting too close to others.

Bugs and Spiders

Just like in our waking life, bugs are pests in dreams too. They represent being bothered or annoyed by other people. Spiders, like mice, represent fears caused by something small or unimportant.

Bugs and Spiders

> I saw little bugs coming out of the corner of the ceiling and then a spider. There was a little black young dog in my room with me.

The room the dreamer is in is her mind. The dog represents her lower, animal self. A person's lower self is their animal like behavior which is based in negative emotions such as fear, jealousy, greed, etc. The dog is young because this is a recent change in her behavior and feelings, or an incident recently occurred to cause these feelings. The ceiling of the room represents her imagination. The bugs mean that she is being bothered by concerns that are basically from her own imagination or of her own creation. The spider represents a particular fear that is causing these thoughts.

Fish

Fish swim around in the element Water, so they represent the feelings swimming around in our subconscious.

Calm water

> Last night I started my dream hearing the father of my child, who I still love, having an argument with someone about him not taking care of our daughter. I dreamt that after the quell he walked pass me and then I walked down to a beach. The water was very calm and clear. I saw my cousin who just recently had a baby sitting on a cliff looking down at the water. She then came to me and wrote the name RANDY on the sand however the water was covering it but it was still visible. After I saw that I was feeding some really lovely fishes in a tank. I saw two of the fishes with jewelry and crowns and the rest looked like angel fishes. In all there could have been about eight fishes in the tank.

Calm water represents calm emotions. This indicates that the dreamer is a person who always stays calm and sees only the best in people. The cousin who just had a baby represents the dreamer's motherly, nurturing, and protective nature. Being on a cliff means that her emotions are very far down, or suppressed. Even though she believes that her daughter is not getting the attention she deserves from the father, she keeps calm and rational. The meaning of the name Randy probably comes from the character on the television show, *My Name is Earl*, which represents someone who can be easily taken advantage of. Thus, the dreamer feels that her calm and peaceful nature allows her to be taken advantage of by the daughter's father.

Looking into a fish tank means that she is starting to pay more attention to her feelings. She may soon be ready to express how she really feels. The fish in the tank are wearing crowns and jewelry because she feels materially satisfied, so maybe she really doesn't really need to complain about anything. The angel fish confirm that she wants to see herself as angelic, and therefore would never want to disturb the peace by expressing anger.

DISHONESTY

> My husband and I were sitting in a room and an old man came and asked, "How are your finances now, because I am happy after some treatment and doing well in business. What about you?" I said, "I am still struggling." The man had taken our money by cheating somehow. He made a face and didn't give our money back. My husband and I were very angry.
>
> Then, we were going home along the beach. The beach was eroded and I was worried about my husband not walking carefully and falling into the sea. Then I saw three rats that were dying. I told my maid to get rid of them.
>
> Next, I saw fish hanging on the wall in a wooden frame. Ants were on the fish. Then I put the fish into the sink to clean for cooking. Then some girls came in and I said, "Wait, I am taking out the fish because you might not be able to tolerate the smell".

It is clear that the dreamer is having trouble trusting people at this time. The dream is showing that she is suspicious of anyone who is doing financially better than her. She believes anyone doing well must be dishonest. The eroding beach indicates that she is worried that because her husband is honest that he will have trouble keeping their finances on solid ground. The dying rats mean that she can't tolerate people who are dishonest and cheating. The smelly fish represent business deals or opportunities that she feels are probably scams. In other words, they smell bad to her. The ants on the fish represent the details, or fine print of the opportunities.

Horses

Horses are energetic and powerful animals. In our dreams they represent our drive and energy.

WILD HORSE
> I had a dream last night that I was driving through a town that looked on the first impression to be abandoned. Suddenly a wild horse came running across the road in front of me. I pulled to the right so I didn't hit it. As I watched, a Jack Russell terrier came running toward the horse. The horse had a rope tied around it and the dog grabbed the rope and jerked on the rope to stop it from terrorizing the people of the town. The dog gave a growl and the horse went running back to where it came from. I got the sense that the horse knew the dog was in charge and the dog was keeping the horse from doing something bad.

> I went to pick up the dog to see if I could find out where he belonged and suddenly an old man drove up in an old truck. He told me it was his dog and had been missing for 5 years. He kept calling the dog him, but the dog was female. I knew he was lying and felt very uneasy about giving the dog back. The man kept insisting it was his dog. I couldn't believe that the dog in fact had been gone for 5 years and was his.

> Suddenly I looked around and there were a few people around that were afraid and sad. They did not like this man and for some reason I could tell that he was the source of their town being in the condition that it was in.

This dream seems to be describing the dreamer's career or work environment. Driving in her dream shows her progress on her life path. According to the dream, where the dreamer is in her life right now is empty and unfulfilling. The horse represents her enthusiasm and energy, drive and ambition. The dog is a terrier which is a symbol for terror. The dog chasing away the horse means that the dreamer's fear, probably fear of failure, is stopping her from giving her all.

The man represents power, like a boss or owner. It could be there is someone like this in her life who dominates through the use of fear and intimidation. The part where he says the dog is his but she doesn't believe him means that she is getting wise to these tactics. By the end of the dream she seems to be ready to abandon her fears and bring back the drive and energy of the horse.

Bears

Seldom are bears the gentle and docile creatures of movies. In our dreams they represent anger and negativity, too big and loud to go unnoticed.

GROWLING BEARS AND DOGS

> I dreamt last night that there were wild dogs and bears attacking the people in my town. I live in a small town. I remember all the howls from the wild dogs and the bears growling, and roaring. There were blood curdling screams coming from the victims that they were attacking. My family and I were running to our truck and we passed some kids who were playing in their front yard like they didn't even hear the horrible noises.

Then we arrived back at our truck. The next thing I know, there's my oldest sister in the back of our truck with my 2 year old daughter. In the cab of the truck there is a man and his wife and kid, along with my youngest sister with her 2 year old boy. I told my husband that I would drive. So, I was running around the front of the truck when I see my husband already in the driver side, and he was backing up and leaving me.

At that point lots of wild dogs and some bears came towards me. So I jumped on the hood and crawled to the back with my sister and baby. When I got back to them, there was a dog growling and about to attack my baby. So I punched it as hard as I could in the head, and knocked it off the truck. The bears were running after us trying to kill us. But we could only move in slow motion. We couldn't get away from them fast enough.

This dream is about the dreamer trying to shelter her children from the negativity between her and her husband. The wild dogs and bears are the two of them arguing and behaving badly toward one another. The kids in the yard don't hear the noises because she feels that children shouldn't have to be aware of their troubles and she pretends that they can't hear. The truck represents trying to keep them away from hearing the arguments, but her husband in the driver seat means that she doesn't feel in control of the situation.

BOYFRIEND'S PRODUCE

In my dream I thought that the guy I'm dating was out of town so... I decided to go to his place and pick some fruits and vegetables from his backyard garden [he doesn't actually have a house, backyard or garden]. I arrive at the back of his house and see him through the window. He is sitting on a couch hanging out, conversing and laughing with two guy friends.

I feel embarrassed because I don't want him to think that I'm stalking him. So I hide, but still work my way to his backyard to pick the produce.

> *The garden is dry and withered. I never actually see any produce. One of his friend's sees me and points me out so I start running away and they chase after me. I am running through plains and jump 2 fences. They start gaining on me. When I get to the 3rd fence, I hear my guy say "she is not going to jump that 3rd fence." In my dream, I'm thinking "oh hell yes, I am". I start to jump the fence then think, "maybe I shouldn't. Maybe I should just stop running and explain my actions to him."*
>
> *But I jump over it and then find myself running through a forest or woods. A small bear attacks me and either scratches or bites my leg. I see blood. Somehow, I escape the bear and my guy and his friend catch up to me. I am back to the plains and my guy is laughing at me, He is not angry and asks me why I ran away. He says that it's ok that I came over, he doesn't mind... I feel relief.*

This dream shows that the dreamer is starting to think about her boyfriend in a new way. Specifically, she is wondering if he would be a good provider. She doubts that he would, since his garden was withered and there was no produce. When she sees him, he is hanging out on the couch with his friends. So, she definitely is concerned that he may be lazy. She runs away in the dream because she doesn't want him to know that she is having these thoughts. The fences represent the fact that although she continues to avoid confronting this issue, it will become increasingly harder as time goes on. The bear attack represents being hurt by this at some point in the future, and she is worried about the argument that it could cause.

Snakes

Snakes generally represent fear and deception. They also appear in dreams where the dreamer is feeling limited or restricted by someone.

SNAKE DREAMS

> *I dreamt of being bitten by a snake while I was walking in a forest... I was slightly afraid but then I relax after it bites me.*
>
> *The next night my boyfriend wakes from having a dream of being bitten by a snake... only this one was a constricting snake (he did not specify a particular snake). In his dream he wakes up in bed and a snake is coiled around his arm so he stays still so it doesn't bite him then before he removes it he falls back asleep, then he wakes up again and the whole thing is wrapped around his body.. He jolts and causes the snake to tighten then bite him.*

By walking through the forest the dreamer is facing her fears of the unknown. Since getting bitten doesn't really bother her that much, this dream shows that she has realized that some of the things she is afraid of are not really that bad at all. This is a positive dream because it shows that she is overcoming fears and becoming more courageous. This shows that she could soon be taking a big step forward in her life because she has let go of fears that are holding her back.

Her boyfriend's dream is about feeling controlled and restricted. When someone dreams about sleeping in bed, they are dreaming about letting their guard down. To fall asleep, we need to relax and trust that we will be safe and secure. The boyfriend dreams that he is attacked by the snake while sleeping. So, he is worried that he is too trusting of someone who will try to do him harm when he is not paying attention. The snake being coiled around his arm means that he is feeling powerless. Most likely, he is relying on someone else who he has trusted and has some power to control his destiny. The boyfriend is concerned that his trust has been misplaced. Waking up and seeing the snake means that he recently noticed something in this other person that is causing his doubts. However, he falls back asleep, meaning he ignores his doubts and continues to rely on this person. He is probably worried about being "bitten" by this person if he says anything. However, when he wakes up again, the snake is now wrapped completely around him. This means that he is afraid that if he doesn't do anything about it, this person will soon have complete power and control, leaving him with none. In this dream, the snake represents the tempter who gets you to trust them and then stabs you in the back.

Having snake dreams? - Someone is being deceptive

Alligators / Crocodiles

As amphibians, alligators and crocodiles live in the water, but can come out on land. This is similar to the way our fears live in the subconscious but can always come out to stop us from living life the way we want. In dreams, they represent fears that are emerging.

ALLIGATORS
I don't remember everything very well but, all I remember is that alligators were trying to eat me and someone else. I did see my husband even though we are no longer together. I don't understand why I would dream of alligators trying to eat me. It really scared me.

Since the ex-husband and another person are in the dream, the dream is probably referring to the dreamer's fears about starting a new relationship. Being eaten refers to being consumed by someone else, or letting a relationship consume her individuality. So her fear is really about the compromise and sacrifice of personal ambitions that often come with sharing your life with another person.

Elephants

Elephants aren't that common in dreams, but when they appear they represent something "big".

ELEPHANT
I dreamt that I looked into the veranda and I saw a baby elephant come in and sit on his bum with his legs sticking out. There were also one or two cats in there as well.

The veranda/porch was not mine, but seemed familiar.

The elephant in this dream is blocking the dreamer's vision of her life path and purpose. Instead of being able to see the view out her veranda, she can only see the elephant. The presence of the cats means that intuitively she knows that she is being distracted. The message of the dream is that she should trust her feelings and follow her intuition. But, instead, something else is taking all her attention. Perhaps she feels if she focuses on this other thing, she will be done with it, and then get back to what she is really supposed to do with her life. However, the elephant is only a baby now. So that means it will soon grow bigger and require even more of her attention.

Sea Lions

Sea lions in dreams should be interpreted as lions of the sea. They swim in the waters of the subconscious waiting to release their ferocious and aggressive energy.

TORNADOES AND AN AQUARIUM
> Last night in a dream with my husband me, my kids and a bunch of other people were running from a huge storm about to hit our area. We ran from house to house, but couldn't find any house that we thought was strong enough to hold out the storm. We can see the multiple tornadoes coming, too numerous to count. We run through the airport, and other businesses, stopping shortly, only to continue on when we realize that the buildings are not strong enough. On the way while running, I hear someone talking, a guy who is running with us. He says but at least now people show kindness. They will offer me crackers where they would offer me nothing before. Anyway, we find our way to the zoo and I look at the sea lions aquarium. I decide that we have finally found a place to weather the storm. We enter in, my husband first, and me holding one of our kids. I notice the water and am afraid I will fall in, and I fear for my child. About the time I step inside the aquarium the storm is over. We walk outside and I immediately feel this comforting warm breeze and see the skies clear in fast motion replaced by the most beautiful things I have ever seen.
>
> As I am basking in the beauty I hear a noise...and I wake up.

The dream represents levels of consciousness. The air represents conscious thoughts, while the water represents subconscious feelings. The tornadoes represent a cleansing of the dreamer's thoughts; like big vacuum cleaners sucking up all the dirt. Too much negative thinking has resulted in holding on to physical things and ideas that are no longer right for her. Although she tries, there is no escaping the cleansing process.

Her dream shows that the only way to escape her reality is to ignore the unpleasant issues by trying to have fun and stimulate only happy feelings. Water represents the realm of emotions, so an Aquarium is a pleasant and safe way to experience them without really getting wet. "Sea" lions represent the potential anger that she could feel if she really allowed herself to feel her true emotions. But instead, she decides to keep out of the water and not acknowledge the truth about her feelings.

The message of the dream is that big changes are happening and she is looking for an escape. She shouldn't be afraid to clean house and let go of whatever needs to be eliminated from her life. Once the storm clears, she will have a new chance to live life without the things she doesn't need.

Chapter 7 – Buildings and Places

When describing a dream, one of the first things people mention is the location or setting. Location is one of the most important symbols in any dream because it establishes the dream context.

Houses / Mansions

Dreaming of a house with many rooms means you are dreaming about your mind. What you keep in each room of the house is the fears and programming that your mind has recorded. Houses with several levels normally represent the levels of one's mind. The basement represents the subconscious and the higher levels represent increasing levels of consciousness.

Demons in the Basement
> *Last night I dreamed that I was staying in a large house with several floors, a complicated room structure and a large basement. I was left alone in the house at night, and went into the basement to work. I became aware of demons who were aware of me and out to do me harm. I had to finish the work in the basement, and not flee the demons. So I began to sing cheerful songs to protect myself—and to appear unafraid. The demons were not able to harm me.*
>
> *Then I needed to go upstairs to get something. As I was walking up to the first floor, I saw a man climbing the stairs to the second floor. I was surprised to see him there because I knew I should be alone in the house. Then I realized he was a robber. At the point I realized that, he turned, saw me, and aimed a gun at me, intending to kill me. I felt fear and surprise. The surprise came because I had had no expectation of this turn of events. There was no escape from the imminent death.*

Then, suddenly, I was on the fourth floor balcony. I had no idea how I had gotten there, but the sudden shift of position had prevented his bullet from hitting me. Two children were with me. Then, suddenly, the robber/murderer was on the balcony with us, intending to kill us. He was standing by the railing. I knew I had to protect the children—so I ran quickly at the man and shoved him over the balcony. He fell to his death. I felt sad that I had had to kill someone, but happy I was able to save myself and the children.

Dreams about mansions are very common. They usually represent one's own mind. As the dreamer moves about the mansion she discovers the thoughts and memories she keeps inside. The basement is a sublevel, so this represents the subconscious. Demons represent the fears that create her nightmares.

Going up the stairs means becoming more aware; more conscious of her fears. The higher the level, the more aware she becomes. This dream is showing her that she needs to let her fears out of the subconscious so she can confront them. The robber in her dream means that she has fears about her personal security. She could be worried about her financial security or her personal safety.

She is able to conquer her fear on the fourth floor, but not on the first/second. This means getting rid of fears is not a simple matter. Simply acknowledging their existence is not enough. She needs to raise them to a higher level of consciousness. This means she needs to look at them in terms of her life purpose. Is getting robbed, mugged, or losing her money part of what she is supposed to experience for a life lesson? If it isn't, then it won't happen. She needs to look at her fears with the realization that she only has the experiences that will teach her what she needs to learn.

HAUNTED HOUSE

I dreamed that my husband was no longer in my life. My 2 year old daughter and I were no longer able to afford our home. My mother accompanied us to look at one where we would be allowed to stay for free. It belonged to an old couple. It was very isolated, out in the woods. It was an old house, two stories, and despite its age it offered all that we needed and was in decent shape.

We were told after entering that the woman and her young baby who lived there previously died in the house, but we were not told any of the background to that. My mother wanted us to leave the house, but I felt a strong need to be in a place where I didn't need to rely on anyone else. The house was full of the things the woman had left in it. I looked at her shoes and hats. The bedrooms were slightly messy. The next thing I know, my mother and I are in the bathroom. I look down and see two footprints in blood. One of an adult, and another of a very small infant. It bothered me greatly, and my mother began to tell me how most spirits don't bother you. I feel afraid and dread the nights in this house ahead of me, but feel I must stay.

Ghosts in dreams usually mean the dreamer is dreaming about fears that are "haunting" her. A part of her is concerned that she is too dependent upon her husband. She feels a bit trapped and vulnerable and perhaps is thinking about getting a job or an income of her own. Her mother is in the dream because staying at home was normal for her generation. The old, isolated house represents living in the old, traditional, manner where the woman was naturally dependent upon her husband. The woman's things being in the house represents the attitude that a woman's place is in the home. It's messy because she is not sure that she wants to continue to accept that.

Being in the bathroom is a symbol for getting rid of the concern of this potential situation. The footprints of blood left by the ghosts means that she is concerned that her role as a housewife and mother could last for an eternity as she spends her whole life doing it.

Apartment

An apartment is similar to a house in meaning. However, sometimes a house or apartment can represent one's physical body.

Moving

> A few nights ago I dreamt that I had to move because they were going to renovate our building. It was being torn down and rebuilt.
>
> I moved into a beautiful apartment and there was an older Russian man living next door who I could see from my window. There was a lady in my apartment holding a bunch of papers and doing some calculations and she said: "Your rent is going to be much lower, $444.00."

In this simple dream, the dreamer is hoping to renovate her body. Like many women, she wants to lose weight. The Russian means "rushing" or being in a hurry. The lady with the calculators or papers is probably referring to her watching her calories.

Skyscrapers

Tall office buildings are often present in dreams about one's career. They represent what you have built up so far in terms of accomplishments and advancement. When children are in the dream, buildings can also represent adults.

Terrorist Plane

> I was sitting on the sofa of my ex live in boyfriend's apartment when I received a certified letter requiring I attend a formal meeting. I vaguely remember understanding that this meeting was an inquest of sorts regarding some type of terrorist activity that I had witnessed.

Chapter 7 – Buildings and Places | 103

I am standing in the back of a large conference room on a top floor of a very tall building. There are floor to ceiling windows on every side. Everyone is in formal business attire. The square conference table in the middle of the floor is full and there are several of us standing in the back of the room. I do not recall any particular person in the room, or what was being said.

At the sound of extremely loud airplane engines all talk ceases and everyone looks to the sky. A few stories below us there is a small, odd shaped plane making slow circles. The plane then looks up and faces us as we watch.

The plane almost looks to have a face. Small eyes and 2 symmetrical tentacles which stick straight out from its face. The place flies upward and hovers level to the window through which we are watching, and seems to look back at us for several seconds.

It then races toward the window and pierces it with its tentacles. It does this 3 times, then flies to the floor below us and does the same. It repeats this action at each floor, heading downward.

After a few seconds of shocked silence, everyone begins to rush toward the exit. This is when I woke.

This dream shows that the dreamer is concerned that other people are becoming jealous of her. She is worried that someone wants to take her down from her high position. She believes that someone may be placing blame on her. The certified letter means that she feels that she has no choice but to face this person's unfair accusations.

The tall building represents the heights to which she has ascended. The formal attire means that she has been very careful to do the right thing and follow protocol. The airplane is at a lower floor, which means that the person who is against her is beneath her in status or position. The face looking at her means that she can sense that she is being watched and scrutinized. Tentacles are also called "feelers", which means that she can feel their scrutiny.

The face plane goes down the floors one by one, because they are digging deeper and deeper into her past and previous history.

Trees / Forest

Woods or forests represent an uncomfortable or strange environment. Dreaming about being in them means being insecure or uneasy. Trees represent growing or the growth process. A tree or roots can represent one's family tree or their family roots.

Growing Up

There was a huge hotel on the left of me. In front of me was a circle of trees and bushes. The trees were more like the pine trees you see in a forest and they were different heights. For some reason I noticed the green of the trees and the brown grass. Then a bear came. It was brown, medium size but, not yet fully grown. It started to chase me so I started running.

I found a tall skinny pine tree and climbed up. The tree started to sway back and forth and I was scared the bear would be able to reach me, so I climbed up higher and the swaying slowed down and then stopped. I could see the circle of trees and there was a brown dirt path around it. On the path was a girl. She asked me where the bear was. I told her it was to the left of her. Which actually it was to the right of her. But, she did run to the left. She screamed and ran because the bear was close behind her. She was running though the little woods they had in front of the hotel. I was watching her being chased.

This is where my dream gets fuzzy. The next thing I was on the ground and talking to a guy. I don't remember about what. Then I was back in the tree and my 10 year old daughter said look mama I have two acorns.

This dream is about the dreamer's daughter growing up. The hotel represents being fully grown, or matured. The trees also represent the process of growing. The bear in the forest represents her fear of the growing process. To avoid the bear, she must climb the tree, which leads to her looking at things from a higher (more mature) perspective. The tree sways because she is inconsistent and conflicted in her feelings about her daughter growing up. The brown path is her daughter's life path. It encircles the trees because she hasn't grown up enough to go off on her own.

The dreamer high up in the tree also represents her role as the parent. She tries to give advice, but she mistakenly tells her to go the wrong the direction. This means that if she lets her fear change her behavior, she may not give her daughter the proper advice she deserves from her parent. Interestingly, the daughter goes the right direction, nevertheless. This means that she will soon be mature enough to make the right decisions for herself, and perhaps not need her mother so much, which is the basic fear of the dreamer.

At the end of the dream the daughter has two acorns, because the dreamer has noticed that breasts are beginning to develop. The dream reveals her desire to hold on to her daughter's childhood by wishing that she doesn't grow up so quickly.

CHRISTMAS TREE

> I was over at my brother's house and asked my sister-in-law why her Christmas tree was still up. It was way after Christmas. She told me that under the tree was a piece of floor missing. So I moved the tree to see what she was talking about. As I moved the tree there was a piece of wood that was cut out in a square. I lifted it and there were squirrels that ran out as I moved the piece of floor.
>
> My niece was so frightened that she ran onto my lap for me to hold her. The weirdest thing is that my niece is 17 and I sure wouldn't be holding her. I do have to say that my brother and I haven't spoken to each other for 3 years now and he is my only

> sibling our parents are passed. We do live in different states but we are only a 5 hour drive from each other. I did visit that state just a month ago but wouldn't dare to stop over. Last time I saw him he got mad at me for a really stupid reason.

The Christmas tree represents two things: the holidays and family gatherings; and your family tree. Underneath the tree is your "roots". Since there is a piece of floor missing, it means that without family in your life, there is a part of you that feels the foundation for your life is incomplete. Squirrels live in trees, so they would represent you and your family back together under your family tree. Your niece being frightened means you would be afraid to contact them again. However, the general message of the dream is that part of you wants to contact your family so you won't be without them for the holidays.

Mall

A shopping mall is a symbol of materialism and economic prosperity.

DRIVING TOWARD MALL

> Mom was driving away in a car towards the mall, at an ungodly hour (2AM), when nothing was open. Nothing was rational about her decision to drive her car at that time. After coming back home shortly after, she irrationally proceeded to drive away again, and crash the car. She returned in a taxi cab. It was like in the dream, you knew something bad was about to happen.

The mall represents the economy and finances and the mother could represent the dreamer's financial future, retirement, investments, etc. A car always represents the progress of one's life. The car crashing means he is worried that his finances will crash and he will lose his savings. The car is gone at the end of the dream. So, this represents that the dreamer doesn't know how he will be able to continue to live if he loses his money.

PLANE CRASH AT MALL

> *I had the strangest dream last night, I was outside of a mall standing in the parking lot, and I saw a low flying plane and the top part of it broke apart, it then nosed dived and crashed into an empty part of the parking lot, it was horrible. I pulled out my cell phone to dial 911, when I flipped it open my friend was on the other line, I told her what happened and I was crying, then I closed the phone and saw the ambulance came. People gathered around the damaged plane and one person survived the crash and was taken into the ambulance.*
>
> *I walked into the mall where I saw another friend. She told me she would see me later and walked away. Then I was in a store with a lot of television sets and there was a news report that showed 2 buildings that had imploded, almost next to each other. Then President Obama walked up with a security person with him, he was watching the news report and turned to me and said that he will make sure this won't happen, he then shook my hand and walked away (another strange thing is that he looked old in my dream and he had a lot of wrinkles on his face.)*
>
> *I then walked around the corner and saw my friend again. She was sitting on a bed watching TV. I asked her to come with me and she said she couldn't because she had to wait for her husband and while she was talking to me she had tears rolling down her face. This is where the dream ended.*

The mall is a symbol for consumer spending and the way the dreamer feels about spending money at this time. The plane falling is a symbol for her concern about the economy crashing. The buildings imploding are about businesses going bankrupt. She is talking to her friends in the dream probably because she has been discussing these fears with them. Together, they are all worried about their financial situations.

President Obama is in this dream because he has tried to reassure everyone that he will be able to bring the economy back. However, the strain on his face in the dream shows that the dreamer remains unconvinced. The friend who is waiting for her husband shows that the dreamer would like to be able to let her husband deal with this so she doesn't have to be worried herself. One good message in the dream is that there was a survivor from the plane crash. This means that she feels it is possible that she may escape this economic situation relatively unharmed.

The dreamer's feedback to this analysis was "I live in a city that is a big manufacturing town and it has taken a lot of hits lately, with plant closures and people losing their jobs. So the economy has been worrying me for awhile now."

Bank

A bank normally represents safety, security and stability.

BANK ROBBERY

I was in a very expensive looking bank in the city. When all of a sudden a man in the line starts waving a gun around. He's wearing a suit with slicked back hair. He darts towards the counter where the only bank teller is and demands her to hand over lots of money. Everyone runs out of the building except for me. I just stand there and watch, feeling quite neutral about it.

The teller starts counting lots of bills one by one to hand it over. The suit robber looks around pedantically making sure no one was coming into the building (the front of which was made of glass looking onto a busy street)

I suggest openly "I think she might be counting the bills slowly because she's waiting for the cops to come because she's secretly pressed a button under the counter to alert them"

Many cop cars arrive. The robber grabs the money and runs into one of the back rooms of the bank. The bank itself is so big that it takes up one block of the city. It has many entrances/exits. The cops surround the blocks and some cops run in and chase him through the back door.

A few more cars show up, vans of different colors waiting at different exits of the bank. I know that these vans are "pick up" points for the robber to flee to safety.

I am intrigued and I run into the back part of the bank to see how the cops are doing. I am still a neutral character in all of this. The back of the bank is full of corridors and glass revolving doors and seemed so big and complex. It was a maze. A couple of cops stop by me and I overhear their conversation "He's still in here somewhere but we haven't found him yet".

"I think he went that way" I say, but I didn't really know. All I knew is that I was such a neutral character that anyone would listen to me and I was having fun with it. They ran off in that direction.

Then my dream changes to me having a family lunch with my good side of the family... Except my grandmother is in a wheelchair in the dream, but not in real life. Everyone is talking and eating/the usual and my grandmother's wheelchair keeps falling over every now and then. When she falls, the noise is large on impact but her face has no expression or movement. When we pick her up she's fine again. It was weird.

The last time she fell in the dream, she tried to go down a step with the wheelchair. When she fell, I looked over and saw my uncle look the opposite way and smirk slightly before we all rushed over to pick her up. This dream felt like the dream sequences out of the TV show Twin Peaks.

A bank represents safety and security. However, too much safety and security can make a person feel trapped and unable to escape. The dream is about the dreamer taking a risk but having difficulty leaving her safe and secure environment. Robbing the bank is a symbol for the part of her that wants to take a risk. The police represent the part of her that wants to keep that other part under control. Outside the bank, the vans represent several different opportunities she could have if she only could get out of the bank. The corridors and maze represent the obstacles she places in her way.

The grandmother dream is also about the way she views risk. The grandmother is not concerned about falling down, in other words, not afraid of failure. The uncle with the smirk represents her concern about looking foolish if she takes crazy risks and keeps failing.

Las Vegas

Some people may think that dreaming about being in Las Vegas is wish fulfillment, but it really represents a risky situation or gamble.

WHAT HAPPENS IN VEGAS...
> *Last night I had a dream that I was in Las Vegas. My daughter was there and her boyfriend. She had gone out to buy something and she came back with a bottle in a shape of a sphere with a stand. If you looked at this bottle it looks like a mushroom (nuclear).*

This dream shows that the dreamer has a problem with her daughter's boyfriend. Being in Las Vegas means that she feels this boyfriend is a gamble. The bottle is the container in which she keeps her true feelings bottled up. However, since it looks like a mushroom cloud, her feelings are about to explode.

Hospital

Dreaming about being in the hospital means you are trying to heal, or recover from, a part of your life that has not gone so well.

IN THE HOSPITAL

Last night, I had a dream where I was in the hospital where I was surrounded by medical staff that was doing medical tests on me. I remember having the IV drip going and the medical staff was doing a lot of blood work on me.

My question is what could this dream mean because I've been having a lot of medical-orientated dreams lately.

The main symbol in this dream is blood. Blood refers to our genetics, specifically, ties to our family. It also refers to what is inside us. The IV drip and blood work symbolize a change in attitudes and beliefs that come from her childhood environment. Perhaps the dreamer is considering taking a very different path in her life than what her parents would have chosen for her.

NICK NOLTE

I dreamt that I was in the hospital. It was chaotic. A couple, (guy and slender dark-haired white girl) fell on top of me while I was lying on the hospital bed, and the girl said she was going to die but that she would be happy before she died.

I was given tranquilizers in the hospital and later, I was with a tall cold-hearted male doctor who looked like Nike Nolte. I was frantically searching for my medical card in my purse. I searched and searched and searched again but didn't find it. I needed it so the doctor could treat me. I discovered I was looking in the wrong purse. Then I found the purse that belongs to me and found my medical card. By that time, I had another doctor. A big Hispanic woman with a round face, nice green eyes and an evil smile, who wanted to perform a lobotomy on me!! She and another dark-haired white girl were preparing for the operation and she was reading a book. She was reading the operational procedure from the book! I fled from her.

> *At another point earlier in the dream, I was in Las Vegas where a couple: a large tall white woman with long dark straggly hair, who wasn't very attractive and who nobody liked except her husband, because she was rude to everyone, and her husband looked like Nick Nolte. They were both obnoxious.*
>
> *Later, I was with my former boss/attorney from years back, who also resembles Nick Nolte. I'm a legal assistant. He, (my former boss) tried to kiss me but I told him I didn't like him in that way. I was telling him something about the big white woman and how nobody liked her except her husband, but that she had a nice smile only for her husband, and that she was showing people in Vegas how to perform sex acts on strangers while her husband watched.*

The "couple" represents a relationship. Since this happens in a hospital, this dream is about trying to recover from being hurt in her current relationship. Since the girl says she is going to die, it means the dreamer thinks that the relationship will be ending soon. The Nick Nolte look-a-likes in this dream represent the way she sees her partner right now—tough and cold-hearted. Her search for her medical card is symbolic for searching for a solution to this situation—a way to make it better. The presence of the woman doctor in the dream suggests that the dreamer has been getting advice from her friends. Advice that she thinks seems crazy and uninformed. This is represented by the lobotomy reference and the fact that the doctor needed to look up the operation in a book.

The part of the dream in Las Vegas means the dreamer thinks ending this relationship would be risky. The unattractive woman means she doesn't see herself as attractive and wonders if she will find someone else who will think she is attractive.

The boss, being the other Nick Nolte man, represents the way she resents being bossed and dominated in this relationship. Her reaction to him and the remainder of the dream shows that she now finds the physical intimacy with him to be very unpleasant and somewhat disgusting.

New York City

New York could mean different things to different people, but if there are also terrorists in the dream, then it represents concerns about a man-made catastrophe in the vein of 9/11.

CHASED BY TERRORISTS
> I had this dream several years ago, but it has always stayed with me. In the dream, I am in NYC. I am in a building on Fifth Avenue. I am not sure if it is a hotel or a department store, but I am in the basement. I see terrorists setting something up (a bomb?) when they see me. They begin to run after me and I am terrified.
>
> The next scene, I am driving in a car speeding away from the terrorists, but they continue to chase me. My father (deceased) and my brother (alive) try to help me. They wave at me from the side of the road. In the next scene, I am at the edge of a field. I hesitate to cross it. A group of young people are in the same area. A young boy approaches me and asks me if I want to go home to my family. I answer yes. He asks me to take his hand and he will help me to get home. I trust him. I take his hand and I wake up in bed next to my husband.

The terrorists in the basement represent fears of loss of personal security. The building represents what the dreamer has built up in this lifetime—her personal and financial security and happiness. At the time she must have felt that there was a possibility of this being threatened. Seeing the terrorists means seeing the possibility that she could be potentially losing her security. She ran from them because she was trying to find a way to outrun a major change or setback in her life.

She was trying to get out in front of a big upheaval by considering making some big change on her own. A real world analogy for this would be when someone thinks they are going to get fired from their job, so they quit. It's about the security we feel when we take control of a situation instead of leaving it up to someone else.

Her father and brother were at the side of the road because she was looking for some support for what may have appeared to some to be a risky or irrational decision.

The field represents emptiness, so the move she was contemplating involved giving up a lot and perhaps cutting back or going without for some time. The young people there represented youthful attitudes; willing to take risks without worrying about the future. Out by the field, she was trying to determine whether she had the courage and willpower to take this risk. Ultimately, she returned "home" to consider this with her conscious mind and perhaps her husband.

Stadium

A stadium represents something opened to the public. Being in a stadium means that something private is being made public.

MURDER, MURDER
Last night I had two dreams which were somehow similar. I only can remember bits and pieces, but want to know what it means.

Dream One:

I was on the run because I knew I killed somebody but didn't know where and who. Suddenly I was shown a shield, like the ones the Vikings had. It was a round shield with those metal pointy cones on it. I was also shown a sword.

Does this mean I killed somebody in a past life or does it mean something totally else?

Dream Two:

Again I was on the run. First I was in some kind of stadium with a large crowd in it. I tried to hide myself because I knew I killed somebody. This time I knew it was done with a knife. I left the stadium and ran away, trying to hide myself and escape capture. This is the only part of the second dream I remembered.

The dreams are about running away from the past.

The person that was killed was the dreamer's past self. This means that he most likely has tried to remake himself, and give his life a new start.

There is something about his past that he wants to keep buried and secret. He has to keep running to keep this from being revealed. The sword and shield represent the defensive posture he takes when someone tries to pry too deeply. The stadium represents the public. So in this second dream he is realizing his fear of his secret past becoming public.

Bathroom

The bathroom represents cleansing. When you dream about a bathroom it often means there is something in your subconscious that needs to be cleaned out.

DAUGHTER'S PICTURES
I am in my daughter's apartment (she isn't home) I am in the bathroom near the tub when I see two rats on the floor near the wall. When they see me they climb up inside the wall. At the baseboard there is a hole in which they go up inside the wall. I get down on my knees to look where they have gone to see how to close up this hole. While I'm on the floor I see their footprints on the floor.

Next, I'm standing in front of what may be a sink (not sure) and next to it is a tall wardrobe. I open the doors and see two large pull out drawers that contains a lot of photographs just kind of tossed in a pile I don't look at any of the pictures and think I will look at some of them later. One of the drawers is broken and I see a nail holding the drawer front to the side panel but it isn't holding properly.

I then look in the other drawer for a washcloth and only find one towel that I take out and begin to fold properly. In the bottom of the drawer is a little bit of crumb like garbage. Next to this wardrobe type piece of furniture is another piece of furniture as large as a refrigerator. Between the two pieces of furniture I see a fire extinguisher hanging on the wall. It is at this time the smoke alarm went off in my home waking me.

This dream is about healing the past. Since the apartment belongs to his daughter, the dreamer has some guilt or worry about his daughter's past. The bathroom indicates that he feels she needs to have some parts of her past cleaned out of her subconscious.

The rats represent those bad feelings and memories from the past that are hiding in the subconscious. Since the rats hide in the walls out of sight, the past hurt is not being discussed. However, the footprints represent the marks that the past has left on the subconscious.

The next part of the dream has a sink which is confirmation that this is about cleansing. The photographs are a symbol of past memories and experiences. The drawer is broken because these past events can no longer be properly contained and are getting ready to spill into the present.

Looking for a washcloth means trying to find a way to clean the past out of the soul. The second wardrobe means that a second person is involved. The crumb in the drawer represents the food for the rats. This is the energy that is being used to keep these things from coming to the surface. Since only a crumb is left, the dreamer has run out of the energy required to continue to keep these things buried.

The dreams are clearly about healing the past by bringing out the truth of what happened in the past and discussing it so the forgiveness can take place. The fire extinguisher represents being able to put out the anger, hate and bitterness.

In a response to this interpretation the dreamer mentioned that he and his wife were heading toward divorce. He was very concerned that his wife had done a lot of emotional harm to their daughter. And that he only continued to stay in the marriage to counter the damage done by the wife.

School

Being back at school appears in a large number of dreams. It is a sign that the dream contains an important life lesson. So, it is not unusual to dream about something happening at school that normally wouldn't.

WEDDINGS
> I dreamt of two people getting married at my school. When the wedding was done, my four year old cousin went inside and took something like a decoration. An old lady grabbed him and rubbed his head. I grabbed him from her and hit her on her head. I then made my cousin hit her on her head too. When the old woman was walking away I saw she was pregnant.

> Then I went in to the house. I saw some of my aunts and cousins. They all were getting ready for my aunt's wedding. I told them about the old lady. My aunt walked me to my room and told me everything is okay. Upon arrival in the room a book rose into the air. My aunt snapped her fingers and it disappeared. Then after that I saw some pastors preaching next to my room and I asked them for a prayer.

There are actually two weddings in this dream. The first one is at a school, so it means there is an important lesson in this dream. The four year old cousin represents youth and innocence. So, this part of the dream is warning the dreamer to avoid serious relationships and marriage until she gets older. The woman rubbing him on the head means that she is being advised to wait until she is more mature. All of the hitting means that she is conflicted about this issue.

The old woman is pregnant because the dreamer wants to wait to get pregnant and not while she is so young. Her aunt getting married is older, and represents that you should wait. The book represents the dreamer's life story, mostly unwritten. It floats in the air because she is thinking about what she will accomplish in this life. It disappears because if she gets married too young she may not fulfill her ambitions. The praying indicates that she is looking for guidance.

Harbor

Located on the edge of water, a harbor represents a safe place from negative emotions.

SAFE HARBOR

> The dream, as far as I can remember started at a harbor of some kind. I'm guessing I had brought my boat there, otherwise why would I be at a harbor? Anyway, the weather started to take a turn for the worst. Instead of heading home I decided to wait it out at the harbor. I kept hearing stories from other people about how a famous boater's wife drove into a hurricane to reach her husband and died. It didn't seem like I knew these people.
>
> At this point I was getting anxious, and wanted somewhere that looked safer to wait out the storm. My dog and I were out looking for this safe place when we came across this day care/nursery place. I remember saying that it hadn't changed

one bit. Well, except that there was an entire wall knocked down. I grabbed one of the blankets that were wedged under the fallen wall. My intent was to wrap my dog in it. Then we reached that harbor again. The dog didn't want to be wrapped up, so she sat on a post and waited there.

Then all of a sudden my gym teacher from high school was there. I really hated him. But for some reason I was relying on him to tell me when the storm would be here and when it had passed. I think I was pretty afraid at this point. But soon enough the storm passed with just one crack of lightning and one clap of thunder...

In this dream the dreamer hears about how dangerous it could be to leave the safety of the harbor when there is a storm. This means venturing away from her safe environment even though there could be risk and danger. The dog represents her lower self, which includes her fears and instincts. The nursery and the blanket represent having her needs taken care of, like a parent does for a small child. The fallen wall means breaking out of that protected environment. Since the dog didn't want to be wrapped in a blanket it means that she instinctively knows that she is too old to still want to be treated like a child. Sitting on a post means trying to look at things in a higher way or a more mature way and show less fear.

The gym teacher probably represents people who have told the dreamer what to do. She likely resents someone telling her what to do. However, she has been told that if you want to be safe, then you have to listen to what others tell you. This is like when parents say "I'm telling you this for your own good."

The dreamer is at a point in her life where she feels she must leave the protection of her parents, and start deciding for herself what is best for her. Although she instinctively knows that she needs to be independent, she is subconsciously hanging on to the safety and protection that her parents provided when she was a child. The dream clearly illustrates that the trade off of staying with her parents is that she has to listen to them.

The dream ends with the storm not being too severe because she realizes on some level that her fears are more imaginary than real. So, it probably is safe to leave.

Warehouse / Garage

A warehouse or garage is where we store our memories.

WAREHOUSE
I had this dream last night. I've forgotten a lot of the contents of the dream since then, but this is just bits and pieces of what sticks out in my mind. I was in, what I believed was, a farmhouse. I was drawing a bath in the upstairs bathroom. I then realized that the water was running over the window and down the wall outside. I wasn't drowning, just watching. I felt panicked. I went to grab a few people who were also staying in the house with me and brought them outside to see the water. I remember pointing to the places on the wall and patting them saying "look there's water here." I can't recall if they believed me or not.

The only other part I remember was in a warehouse type place. It was cold with concrete floors. All the people that were in the house, I assumed, were there with me in the warehouse. I was under a car checking something out, the gas tank or something I think. Then a man appears out of the corner of my eye. He was wearing what looked to be something Indiana Jones would wear. Hanging in the window, he said to me something along the lines of 'Nothing is as it appears.' Then everyone's faces were smiling at me innocently, then shifted to menacing and frightening. I was scared and cold lying on the ground. They started shouting, "She did it! She did it!" Which then, in turn, I shot up out of bed, feeling like I had been screaming.

The house is the dreamer. Since it is a farmhouse it means that she is still growing and maturing, because a farm is where things are grown. Water represents emotions, and the window represents her eyes, so the whole part about the water running out the window represents crying, or emotional release. There is so much emotion that she can no longer keep her feelings to herself. But when she tries to show the people in the dream the water, she is not sure if they see it. That means that she is not sure that they will think her feelings are valid.

A warehouse is where things are stored, so it represents memory. A car would represent moving forward with her life, but in this dream it needs repairs and isn't going anywhere. The Indiana Jones guy represents adventure that takes her away from home. Again the window symbol comes back and the message she get says that she is not seeing things clearly. The rest of the dream says that the problem is that she doesn't want people accusing her of doing something bad, just because she wants to take off on her own adventure.

CHAPTER 8 – EVERYTHING ELSE

Health Dreams

In essence, every dream can be considered a "health" dream, since they are vital to keeping us healthy and balanced. An awareness of one's subconscious leads to a balanced psyche. Imbalances create inner conflicts which can lead to health problems.

Sometimes, though, the meaning of a dream has to do directly with a health issue. It is often said that the best doctor is oneself. Part of the reason for this is that the subconscious is aware of any imbalances with the body and mind and the resulting health problems.

If you are about to get sick there is a good chance you will dream about it first.

The dreams in this section at first appear to be rather ordinary. However, in each case they were linked to an ongoing health problem or one on the horizon.

History Repeating Itself

It begins with my husband and I debating the best route to get somewhere. I suggest taking a bus, but we realize it's Sunday and buses run infrequently. So we decide to drive our car. We are not living in our current place, but in a city—possibly Philadelphia, but I am not sure of that. We go to wherever we were going, and, on our way home, on the block we live on, we pass a house in which they have many books they are throwing away. We stop to trash pick through the books, and find a number we like. Then I find a box with a number of handwritten diaries—and I put them in my pockets to read later.

We get back in the car to keep driving home. Suddenly I disappear from the car and reappear on the same city block but it looks different. I am standing outside a store. The car is nowhere in sight. I start talking to a woman, trying to figure out what has happened—and point out where I used to live, but someone else lives there now. She says she thinks she remembers me—that I moved out five days after she moved in— back in 67. I say that couldn't have been true because I was a child then. A little later, I learn it is now 2099—and someone else had moved out in 2067. I realize the owner of the diaries was a witch, had seen me take the diaries, and had thrown me into the future. The woman I was talking to led me to another woman who said she got get me back to my time— and gave me something to drink.. When I finished the drink, I instantly went backward in time, but ended up in 2011 instead of 2009. I spent a few hours locating my husband and son's new apartment—and entered. My son recognized me and accepted me when I explained what had happened, but said he didn't think my husband would believe it was me. My husband was sleep. I said, "Leave it to me. I will be able to explain it—- and he will accept me." I then woke him and started telling him what had happened. I showed him the diaries I still had in my pockets as proof. He was crying to see me. Then I woke up.

The books and diaries represent the recording of past events, in other words, history. The reference to a bus and being in a city suggests events that happen to a large group of people, and not just the dreamer. However, since she ends up driving in her car, it means ultimately that this does concern mostly just her. Then there appears to be confusion about time and whether this is the past or the future. The time confusion indicates that this is about history repeating itself. She is concerned that events from the past could be recurring. She ends up two years in the future, which basically just means the near future. So, in a nutshell, her dream is about the feeling that events from the past could be recurring soon.

The meaning of this dream became clearer when the dreamer replied that she is a cancer survivor and health problems have recently had her worried that her cancer could be returning.

Explosion from the Sea

> I had a very vivid dream last night. I was standing in a room which was quite high. I was looking out of the window across to tall buildings and houses. All of a sudden there was a huge explosion and I screamed. I ran in to another room and saw that it was actually coming out of the sea!! There was what looked like lava coming out high above sea level. I ran outside to see what was going on and there were ambulances and people everywhere. I was in what looked like a built up cul-de-sac area, very tropical looking (I have never been here before). There were kids walking around in their trunks that had just been swimming. They were very brown (tanned) so I am assuming local boys. What has struck me most about this dream is the Ambulance. I haven't seen one like this before. It was chunky, red and white and had colored lights around the top. It was not square, it was rounded. I also got a name. Bill Young???!!

This dream is about stress and its physical effects on the dreamer. The ocean represents the dreamer's emotions and the lava indicates anxiety, like when pressure builds up in the earth's crust before it explodes. The ambulances indicate that her health is bring affected. We normally carry emotional stress in our abdomen. So, stress commonly leads to digestive problems. The ambulance is rounded because it represents medication, like a pill. This is probably an antacid or something similar. The tropical setting means that the dreamer needs a vacation or someway to address the stress. "Bill" could be referring to the pill I mentioned, and "Young" means that she may feel that she is too young to be having problems like this.

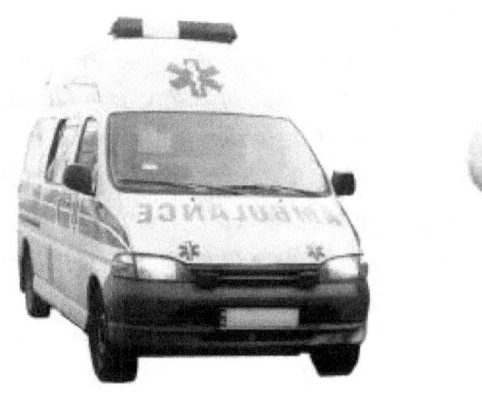

Teeth Falling Out
> *I felt loose teeth with my tongue, and continued to push at them until they came out and I spit them into my hand.*

This is a very common dream that is probably responsible for many trips to the dentist. However, like most dreams, the literal interpretation is not the correct one.

Teeth falling out is a dream that shows lack of self confidence. It shows the inability to sink your teeth into a new challenge or situation.

Food Dreams

Food is very connected to our emotions. We don't just eat to satisfy physical cravings, but to satisfy emotional ones as well.

Fast Food
> *I was inside a fast-food restaurant with good lighting. I could see every area of the restaurant. I think I had just eaten and was snacking on some Doritos. What was strange though was in that one pack there was guacamole, BBQ, and original, in the bag at the same time. My friends and I were all at the restaurant. We had all eaten and were just laughing and interacting, and one person (I know her face but she's a*

classmate) who had not eaten while we were, changed her mind and bought some food. I think it was McDonald's we were all eating. She then asked if we would wait on her so she could eat it there. I said yes. We all walked off with large brown paper bags with the McDonald's logo. They weren't heavy though and we carried them with one hand.

I never saw the faces of the group of friends I was around, but I was very relieved and happy and had a free and overall ecstatic joyous feeling. Then we all took seats. Someone sat across from me at a two seater table while I proceeded to sit in a guy's lap at the table and he made space for me to sit between his legs and he was hugging and kissing me so I think it would be my boyfriend, (but I have no boyfriend at the moment). The energy between the both of us was that of comfort and understanding it was real and genuine and very playful. I was laughing and he was too, he was swinging the chair from left to right so the both of us were just playing in the seat. And that's where the dream ended into another dream of me following some friends to get some business done with members of my work group. We got it done but it was a chaotic process. But the main focus is the guy in my dream, my heart was happy and believed it was real.

Snacking and fast food means that the dreamer is looking to satisfy a craving. However, the craving is not one that food can satisfy, because it is for a boyfriend. The two different types of Doritos mixed together means that she is not being careful to eat healthy food. The brown bags of food indicate that she is putting on weight as a result. Her school friend represents the part of her that sometimes shows the willpower to stop from overeating. However, she eventually gives in. She feels happy in the dream, because the food gives her a temporary good feeling that seems like it satisfies her craving. However, the food can't satisfy her desire for a boyfriend who appears in the next part of the dream. So, the message is that she wants a boyfriend, but while she is waiting for him, she is letting food take his place.

The second dream shows that she is letting the whole food/boyfriend thing become a distraction from getting her work done.

CHEESECAKE

> I dreamed that I was eating cheese cake which is a cake that I don't like because it's too sweet but I took a try and I really liked it. I purchased the whole cake and kept eating and it never finished.

When you eat something in a dream it often means that you are about to "swallow" or accept something new. So this dream is telling the dreamer that something she resisted accepting in the past now seems good to her.

FRIEND'S HAMBURGER DREAM

> My friend had a dream that we were at a restaurant and ordered hamburgers and I got served a hamburger but it was upside down and it made me really sad.

The friend (the dreamer) probably sees her friend (the one who sent in the dream) as someone who knows what she wants in life. The dreamer probably doesn't, so she dreams about her friend not getting what she wants. Her hamburger is upside down. This helps the dreamer to feel that it's okay to not know what she wants for her life.

Word Phrases

Dreams are made up of symbols. The messages we get aren't normally words or sentences. Wouldn't it be nice if we fell asleep and our dream was just a sentence that said, "You are worried about losing your job." The reason that doesn't happen is that dreams are emotion-based. When you dream you are feeling the emotions of your subconscious. You can't feel a sentence.

However, words and word phrases can occur in dreams alongside other symbols. In some dreams, the dreamer is handed a note or they are given a name.

Some examples from dreams in this book are:

"Billy" the snake = a bully

"Skip" the animal expert = skipping out

"Bill Young" = too young to rely on a pill

TAYLOR WILSON

I was in this hotel. It wasn't very nice. I was having a shower and I remember thinking how dirty it was. Afterwards I looked at the time and it said 7am. I went to go and have breakfast at this cafe and ordered toasted rolls with butter and jam, but then I didn't eat them. I don't remember much after this but remember a man writing the name 'Taylor Wilson' on a bit of paper.

Last night I dreamt I was in a hotel again (the hotel was nicer this time) and I met a young boy called Pike who had been out in a corn field picking with his Mother. He only looked about 7 or 8 years old. I also remember the numbers 59, 27 and 83. 27 and 83 were room numbers. I can't remember what 59 was all about, but I just remember the number.

I remember being given a key to what I thought was room 27 and I remember being in this room with my husband thinking that the bed was too small for us. I then remember looking at the key and reading the number 83, so then realized we were in the wrong room and should be higher up.

Dreaming about a series of numbers almost always means the dreamer is a lottery player. Some people believe it is possible to get the winning lottery numbers in their dream. This sort of dream is basically wish fulfillment. The dreamer really wants to be given the lottery numbers, so their subconscious gives them numbers. I don't know how many people win this way, but I have not heard of this happening very often.

The dirty hotel means she is not happy with her present living conditions. Since it is a hotel, she believes that this is a temporary situation. The bread is another symbol for money. She doesn't eat it because she is not currently making much money.

The name on the paper is Taylor Wilson. Taylor Wilson is the name of an actress who is not particularly well known. So, it is doubtful that the actress has any meaning for the dreamer. This is a clue that the name itself is actually a message.

Taylor = "Tell Her"

Wilson = "Will Soon"

7 am = lucky number seven

So, the phrase is, "Tell her she will soon be lucky".

The hotel from the second dream is nicer. This is because in this dream she dreams about the numbers and believe this will change her circumstances. The numbers are the "key" to her moving up financially.

After this interpretation, the dreamer responded excitedly that indeed she is a lottery player and plays the large jackpot drawings twice a week. And, she does consider seven to be her lucky number.

So far, no word on whether she is now a millionaire…

Index of Dream Symbols

affair, 16
air, 21, 27, 36, 72, 85, 96, 117, 118
airplane, 15, 26, 27, 31, 36, 37, 102, 103, 104, 107, 108
altar, 70
ambulance, 107, 125
angel, 44, 62, 87, 88
animals, 27, 48, 77, 83, 85, 89
   alligator, 94, 95
   bear, 90, 91, 92, 104, 105
   bird, 51
   cat, 80, 81, 84, 95
   cougar, 83
   dog, 29, 77, 78, 79, 80, 84, 85, 87, 89, 90, 91, 118, 119
   fish, 13, 87, 88, 89
   insect, 86, 87
   lion, 81, 82, 96, 97
   mice, 86
   owl, 86
   rat, 86, 88, 89, 115, 116
   sea lions, 96
   snake, 48, 92, 93, 94, 129
   spider, 86, 87
   squirrel, 105, 106
   tiger, 51, 81, 84, 85
apartment, 83, 102, 115, 116, 124
aquarium, 96
baby, 49, 50, 56, 57, 58, 65, 69, 73, 87, 88, 91, 95, 96, 101
bags, 26, 127
bank, 108, 109
basement, 72, 74, 99, 100, 113
bath, 80, 120

bathroom, 71, 72, 101, 115, 116, 120
beach, 28, 87, 88, 89
bed, 15, 43, 52, 73, 74, 93, 107, 111, 113, 120, 129
bedroom, 52, 83
blanket, 119
blood, 40, 73, 90, 92, 101, 111
boat, 31, 37, 38, 118
book, 9, 10, 11, 15, 19, 20, 32, 65, 66, 82, 111, 112, 117, 118, 122, 124, 129
boss, 61, 62, 71, 90, 112
bottle, 110
bridge, 9, 10, 21, 22
brush, 44
bullet, 17, 66, 120
bus, 58, 59, 123, 124
camera, 44
car, 14, 20, 31, 32, 33, 34, 36, 37, 42, 47, 52, 53, 61, 63, 64, 67, 68, 79, 80, 106, 108, 113, 120, 123, 124
   parked, 31, 34, 47, 63, 64
cave, 41, 42, 43
cd, 32
ceiling, 47, 49, 87, 103
celebrities, 65, 66, 68, 84, 118
chicken, 13, 70
children, 16, 29, 38, 58, 59, 60, 61, 69, 84, 91, 100, 102
christmas, 41, 105, 106
church, 45, 69, 71
cliff, 79, 87, 88
closet, 65, 66, 69, 72, 73, 74
clothes, 34, 45, 50, 67
clouds, 27
coins, 25, 26, 41, 69, 70
colors

black, 42, 44, 51, 52, 63, 64, 78, 81, 86, 87
blue, 40, 41, 46, 48, 69, 70, 73, 75, 84
brown, 33, 63, 78, 104, 105, 125, 127
burgundy, 40, 41, 42
green, 45, 46, 47, 72, 73, 74, 75, 84, 104, 111
indigo, 48
orange, 42, 43
pink, 45, 46
purple, 48, 49, 52, 69
red, 33, 34, 37, 40, 41, 52, 63, 69, 72, 74, 79, 125
violet, 48, 49
white, 27, 37, 43, 47, 49, 50, 51, 52, 70, 72, 73, 74, 79, 81, 84, 86, 111, 112, 125
yellow, 44, 69
computer, 14, 32, 36
construction, 42
contract, 84
control, remote, 62, 63, 64
couch, 45, 56, 72, 73, 74, 91, 92, 102
crumb, 116
dead people, 9, 51, 67, 68, 69
demon, 99, 100
diamond, 42
diary, 123, 124
dirt, 25, 26, 97, 104
dirty, 21, 24, 25, 26, 38, 63, 129, 130
dock, 28
doctor, 56, 111, 112, 123
door, 26, 50, 59, 60, 63, 73, 74, 78, 79, 81, 83, 102, 109, 116
dorm, 81
drawer, 116
dress, 43, 50, 69
driving, 24, 31, 32, 36, 37, 42, 58, 66, 89, 90, 106, 113, 123, 124
earth, 21, 25, 125
earthquake, 25, 46
eaves, 73, 75
emergency room, 52
extinguisher, fire, 116, 117
factory, 40
farm, 120
fence, 84, 85, 92
fetus, 56, 57
field, 113, 114, 129
fire, 21, 28, 29, 82, 116, 117
fire engine, 28
flower, 44
fluid, 34, 40
flying, 15, 17, 36, 86, 107
food, 70, 116, 126, 127, 128
football, 73, 74
footprints, 101, 115, 116
forest, 92, 93, 101, 104, 105
furniture, 116
game, 36, 50, 51
garage, 68, 120
garbage, 26, 61, 116, 120, 123
ghost, 101
gold, 26, 41
gum, 46
gun, 17, 63, 66, 82, 120
hairdresser, 67
harbor, 118, 119
hat, 21, 36, 70, 101
hole, 41, 86, 115
horse, 65, 89, 90
horseshoe, 66
hospital, 66, 110, 111, 112
hotel, 51, 52, 74, 104, 105, 113, 129, 130

house, 25, 28, 56, 57, 58, 59, 60, 72, 73, 74, 78, 81, 82, 84, 85, 91, 96, 97, 99, 100, 101, 102, 105, 117, 120, 123
jewelry, 62, 87, 88
killer, 26
kissing, 18, 127
kitchen, 28, 70, 82, 83
knife, 115
las vegas, 110, 112
lightning, 86, 119
los angeles, 62
lottery, 40, 41, 129, 130
mall, 65, 66, 106, 107
mansion, 58, 59, 100
mirror, 15, 18, 22, 23
money, 25, 26, 40, 41, 42, 47, 50, 51, 60, 65, 69, 70, 88, 100, 106, 107, 108, 130
mouth, 49, 57, 72, 79
nazis, 71
new york, 113
numbers, 129, 130
oil, 46, 47
papers, 83, 84, 102
photographs, 15, 34, 59, 115, 116
picnic, 49
plaque, 68
police, 56, 69, 72, 73, 74, 108, 109, 110
politician, 35, 107, 108
pregnancy, 56, 57, 70, 117, 118
priest, 45
remote, 62, 63, 64
ring, 41, 42, 62
road, 24, 26, 31, 32, 36, 42, 43, 48, 61, 79, 89, 113, 114
roadblock, 61
robber, 99, 100, 108
rocks, 31, 32
roots, 104, 106
rope, 89
russian, 57, 58, 102
scar, 41, 49, 50
school, 40, 49, 58, 68, 72, 81, 82, 117, 118, 119, 127
shield, 114, 115
shoes, 45, 101
shot, getting, 17, 66, 120
shower, 16, 49, 75, 129
sidewalk, 49
sign, 21, 40, 47, 51, 71, 83, 117
sink, 88, 116, 126
skyscraper, 102
soldier, 70
stadium, 114, 115
stage, 19, 47
stairs, 59, 72, 73, 99, 100
store, 45, 50, 107, 113, 120, 124
storm, 96, 97, 118, 119, 120
streets, 14, 24, 26, 31, 32, 33, 34, 36, 42, 43, 48, 61, 63, 79, 89, 108, 113, 114
stripes, 51, 72, 81, 85
subway, 35
sword, 70, 114, 115
table, 69, 83, 84, 103, 127
taxi, 106
tea, 62
teacher, 119
teeth, 126
television, 15, 20, 65, 72, 73, 74, 88, 107, 109
tentacles, 103, 104
terrorist, 102, 113
throat, 46, 48, 80
tornado, 27

traffic, 33, 36, 42, 45, 66, 71
traffic light, 33, 45, 63
train, 31, 34, 35, 77
treasure, 41, 42
trees, 92, 93, 101, 104, 105, 106
truck, 89, 90, 91
van, 66
vegetables, 91, 92
volcano, 125
wall, 41, 61, 68, 70, 86, 88, 115, 116, 119, 120
wardrobe, 116
warehouse, 63, 120
washcloth, 116

water, 20, 21, 22, 23, 24, 28, 37, 38, 46, 47, 59, 61, 72, 80, 87, 94, 96, 97, 118, 120
canal, 46
ocean, 125
rain, 74
sea, 88, 96, 97, 125
stream, 31, 32, 46
wave, 33, 61, 113
wedding, 69, 70, 117
wheelbarrow, 25, 26
wheelchair, 109
wind, 43, 71, 73, 75, 96
window, 32, 35, 50, 63, 71, 72, 73, 91, 102, 103, 120, 125
womb, 43, 57

www.ingramcontent.com/pod-product-compliance
Lightning Source LLC
LaVergne TN
LVHW051500070426
835507LV00022B/2862